CINDY STEWART

GOD'S DREAM FOR YOUR LIFE

Live Your Life without Limits!

GOD'S
DREAM
FOR YOUR
LIFE

GOD'S DREAM FOR YOUR LIFE
Copyright © 2018 Cynthia Stewart

ISBN:

ENDORSEMENTS

In this dynamic, power-packed book, you will learn the secrets to tapping into *God's Dream for Your Life* and unleash your miraculous potential. If you have ever asked the question, "Is there more?", then this is the book for you. This is a prophetic manual that will activate you and equip you to release your potential and attain God's highest and best for your life.

DR. KYNAN BRIDGES
BESTSELLING AUTHOR, *90 DAYS OF POWER PRAYER*
PASTOR, GRACE AND PEACE GLOBAL FELLOWSHIP

God's Dream For Your Life releases revelation of spiritual things of another realm far superior to ours. Cindy blends the two realms together – spirit and worldly – giving the reader an opportunity to grow and mature with the originator of both, our heavenly Father, Jesus, and Holy Spirit.

KAREN-ELISABETH WILLIAMS,
PASTOR AT THE GATHERING WITH JESUS

Dr. Cindy Stewart is a stellar woman of God, filled with virtue, anointed with God's Spirit, and empowered by love. *God's Dream for Your Life* will refresh, provoke and enlighten you, giving you opportunity to build a glorious path for your future.

DR. PATRICIA KING
FOUNDER OF PATRICIA KING MINISTRIES
CO-FOUNDER OF XPMEDIA

I have been an observer of Cindy Stewart's passion for life and compassion for others, and I am a fan of her love for Christ and His purposes in these days. *God's Dream for Your Life* was birthed in her passionate desire for others to live life from that place of oneness in Christ. In John 14:20, Jesus says, "In that day you will know that I am in My Father, and you in Me and I in you." What a place to live in!

God's Dream for Your Life unveils a supernatural view of the world as declared by Jesus: Christ in us, and us in Him. From our oneness with Him comes the ability to move into His world, allowing Him to make the impossible, in our world, become possible. With transparency and empathy she introduces the reader to the power and wonder of oneness with Christ.

This book is not a book of theory or bland theology. It is personal and prophetic. It is a truth you need to hear, a truth you need to receive. The truth revealed in her books comes from her own personal experiences and success and it will give you a new set of eyes through which you can see the world in a brand-new way.

Don Milam,
Acquisitions Consultant,
Whitaker House Publishers
Author, *The Ancient Language of Eden*

God's Dream for Your Life will bring clarity to your purpose while unlocking vision of what's possible with God.

Cindy's candid testimonies will help you overcome self-doubt and fear of failure to achieve what matters – fulfilling the fullness of God's plan for your life.

Brandi Belt,
Overflow Global Ministries
Cincinnati, Ohio

In *God's Dream for Your Life* Cindy Stewart has created a vehicle that will help navigate you into a life of fulfilling purpose. Drawing from her own journey and the accounts of others, Cindy shows you how to live from the wholeness of heaven. Practical tips and powerful advice will engage you in activities that cultivate healing and provision for you and for others. Not only will you find purpose and direction in these pages, but perhaps more importantly, your God-given identity as well. It's time to dream with God!

ROB & ALISS CRESSWELL,
AUTHORS OF *THE THREEFOLD MIRACLE MANDATE* AND *THE NORMAL SUPERNATURAL CHRISTIAN LIFE*
ALISSCRESSWELL.COM

In *God's Dream For Your Life,* Cindy Stewart has opened her heart allowing you to experience the various and glorious dimensions of dreaming with God. In these pages you will discover what God has always known about you transcends what you have ever known about Him. Cindy intimately shares from her own journey the exhilarating encounters she has had with God and how her life has been transformed by accepting God's invitation to dream His Dream. Lean in and allow "His mighty power at work within you to do far more than you would ever dare to ask or even dream of—infinitely beyond our highest prayers, desires, thoughts, or hopes."

DR. RANDALL WORLEY
AUTHOR OF *BRUSHSTROKES OF GRACE* AND *WANDERING AND WONDERING*
WWW.RANDALLWORLEYMINISTRIES.COM

Have you ever wondered what God thinks about you? Do you know that God formed and created you for this exact time in history? My friend, Cindy Stewart, skillfully answers these questions in her new book, *God's Dream for Your Life*. Each chapter unfolds another dream of God's heart for you, giving insight and encouragement straight from the Word and her own personal life testimonies. This is a timely book that will awaken your heart again for God's big Dream for you.

JULIE MEYER,
INTOTHERIVER.NET
AUTHOR OF SINGING THE SCRIPTURES

TABLE OF CONTENTS

Chapter 1

GOD DREAMS ABOUT YOU

"When God wants to work in your life, He'll always gives you a dream—about yourself, about what He wants you to do, about how He's going to use your life to impact the world." —Rick Warren[1]

---

[1] http://rickwarrenquotes.blogspot.com/2011/03/god-sized-dreams-and-dreaming.html 101217

Did you know that God dreams?

He dreams about you!

He dreams of you walking in your identity as His son or His daughter.

He dreams of you being His friend.

He dreams of you fulfilling your purpose.

He dreams of you being a part of His army.

He dreams of you bringing Heaven to Earth.

He dreams of you as His-story maker.

He dreams of you preparing the next generation.

He dreams of you leaving an inheritance.

He dreams of you spending eternity with Him.

God has dreams for each one of us. In God's eyes, we were not born haphazardly, unplanned or without purpose or relevance on this earth. Every person has a design and destiny for their life that will leave a footprint long after they are gone. God's desire is for each of us to leave a footprint that is one with His. He gives us proof that this is possible in His Word and through the lives of others. We see and experience this both in history and personally through those He sends to encourage and influence us individually along the way.

Listen to the dream God had for Jeremiah:

"Before I formed you in the womb, I knew you; before you were born I sanctified you; I ordained you a prophet to the nations" (Jeremiah 1:5 NKJV).

Allow me to use the words God spoke to Jeremiah to prophetically release God's dream for your life.

"Before I placed you inside your mother's womb, I knew every aspect of you; I knew your heart and all the things you would desire, your design and how it would forge a path to accomplish your purpose. You were created out of My love and as I formed you, My heart was filled with an overflowing, everlasting love for you. I marked you as holy, setting you apart for the extraordinary life I planned for you. When you were born, I planted this truth deep inside you. Your life has intrinsic value to Me and you were made for greatness."

God ingrains purpose in each one of us before we are born. Our purpose begins to crystallize and becomes clearer once we choose to be part of the Family of God. I remember when I was in my teens and my grandmother wanted to send me to a Christian

Bible college; but I rebuffed her offer. Though I had accepted the Lord at an early age, my life with Christ was interpreted by others' opinions and my sporadic church attendance, not through a daily walk with Him. I really did not understand my purpose and frankly, it took me many years to discover God's purpose for my life. You can read about the outcome in "My Journey with Jesus" at the end of this book.

Dream and Purpose

Many of you, too, will find your purpose becoming clearer as you grow in your relationship with God.

As we talk more about purpose, we are honing in on why you and I were created; in essence, why we exist. One of our core purposes for which we exist is for the love and pleasure of our Heavenly Father. We are important to Him as His creation, His family, and His children; and additionally, we are also important in terms of how His Kingdom operates on earth.

As we address God's dream for you – and each one of us –, it is helpful to understand what a dream is in order to fully grasp how God has put His dream and purpose together. A dream is an aspiration, an intention, and a desire. God's dream involves His best inviting you to partner with Him in your purpose.

What is your purpose? A purpose is the reason you were created. You were created because you are God's dream – His aspiration, His intention, and His desire.

Let me introduce what might be a new idea to you. Have you ever thought about partnering with God for your dreams? What a thrill it would be to join forces with God to make your dreams come true? God is a dream giver and He is a dream fulfiller. Our dreams come alive as we spend time with the Lord. He unfolds things we think are impossible and they suddenly become possible!

We hear testimonies about this all the time. Following is a life-changing testimony from Tom.

I was born in 1975 to parents who fought all the time. By the time I was ten, my parents divorced. For the next four years, I was sent back and forth between parents. Mother had an alcohol and drug addiction and disappeared when I was fourteen. I caused problems at home until I was kicked out shortly before I turned sixteen. I started drinking and using drugs at seventeen. I was in and out of jail all the time; arrested over twenty times from age seventeen to twenty. At twenty, I was arrested and sentenced to two years of prison with eight years of probation, after facing the possibility of a 40-year sentence. I reconnected with my Father while incarcerated and my aunt visited twice a month to encourage me and talk about the Bible. After getting out of prison, I began to play music again in church. At that time, I rebuilt my relationship with the Father, and built a strong bond. I met and married my wife and continued to serve in music ministry in churches. I worked in the cabinet industry for over fifteen years, working tirelessly trying to make ends meet. I never felt like I got paid for the true value of the work that I did. I was doing high-end custom finishing for low-end pay.

I began to attend the Gathering with Jesus at the Gathering Apostolic Center and after faithfully tithing, God began to change things in my life. I was prophesied that God was going to give me increase and promotions, but I was used to being undervalued at work because I thought I was being punished for my past. When I finally let go of the past, God quickly began to change the future. I was recruited by a Fortune 500 company and put in a position to train people all across the state in cabinet shops. I began to use the skills I thought were undervalued and underused to teach people the skills I had learned and mastered. God has continued to work in my life and the life of my family, showering us with favor and blessing. – *Tom*

Once The Gathering Apostolic Center witnessed this breakthrough in Tom's career, we began to see more and more people move into their dream careers. Then we began to have breakthroughs in families that became restored. Within a few months, four families who were estranged from their adult children and had not spoken in years were restored; one family was going on nineteen years without speaking and God restored their relationship! God is amazing. It is His heart's desire that we live in His fullness while on this earth. Jesus said, "I have come that they may have life, and that they may have it more abundantly" (John 10:10 NKJV).

When I talk on the subject of dreaming God's dreams, I share the story of Solomon in 1 Kings 3. Solomon had become king at a very young age. He went to Gibeon to offer sacrifice to the Lord, and God appeared to him in a dream. God said to Solomon in this dream, "Ask! What shall I give you?" As we read further, we see Solomon asked for God's heart to lead the people.

Solomon had seen the devotion of his father, David. Solomon's heart had been prepared for the question long before

God asked it. The life he lived as a child revolved around serving God. Not all have had this lineage; some of us are first-generation believers who are now raising our children to love and serve God.

As born-again believers in pursuit of God, we can set our heart's desire to align with what He desires. Whether our dream is to write books to reach others for Christ, or our dream is to own a business that brings jobs and finances to others or a dream to have a home – God fulfills those dreams. Whatever it is, God honors our dreams. Jesus tells us four times in John 14-16 to ask and it will be given to us; this includes asking for what we desire. DREAM BIG with GOD and trust Him to guide your dreams, weeding out the dreams that are not His best for you. Trust that He will steer you toward the dreams that are not only the best for you, but for His Kingdom.

Setting Your Heart toward Dreaming

When you begin to dream with God, be specific. Not only ask Him to join in your dreams, but also learn to partner with Him in dreaming. When we partner with God, it opens up endless possibilities for our dreams to be fulfilled. He created you with the ability to dream and deposited infinite possibilities in your heart. It is important for you to discover what God has put in your heart.

Start by giving yourself permission to dream the impossible and begin to imagine what your dream would look like fulfilled. Our imagination is important to dreaming. With our imaginations, we are able to see our dreams come alive. "For as he thinks in his heart, so is he" (Proverb 23:7 NKJV). We have been afraid of using our imagination because we have not understood the power and gift of our sanctified imagination. Scripture instructs us to throw down any imagination that sets itself above God. It does not say we are not to use our imagination. Our imagination is found within our mind, and our mind is set apart, sanctified; we have the mind of Christ revealed to us by the Holy Spirit.

Our imagination is a tool we can use to picture the goals ahead. Here is a great example of the power of using our imagination. Dr. Cho, pastor of the largest church in South Korea, brought his dream into reality by using his imagination.

For months, he had only five people attending services in the little tent, and one of these was his girlfriend! Nonetheless, he preached loudly and intensely, causing his girlfriend to ask him, "Why are you preaching so loudly? You're hurting our ears!" Dr. Cho answered, "Because I'm not preaching only to you five. I'm preaching to the 300 that I see."

Finally, after two years, the 300 started coming. Then Dr. Cho said, "God, I'm not happy with just 300. Let's go to 3,000." Then he went to 50,000, 100,000, 200,000, and more! When I was with this dynamic man, his church numbered at around 200,000 people. He said, "I'm going to half a million!" Then, when they reached half a million, he took a long vacation with his dear wife. While he was away, he said, "Lord, we accomplished it. Now, I'm going to retire. I want to spend a lot of time golfing and going to other countries." The Holy Spirit responded, "No you don't. We're going to a million!" Now the church ministers to over a million people through satellite churches, and Dr. Cho has 750,000 in his Seoul, Korea congregation. This great leader told me, 'I've had thousands of poverty-stricken

Koreans come who are millionaires today, because they looked at the Cross and they saw the spotted and speckled blood of Jesus Christ, and they prayed and imagined until their prayers became prayers of faith." [2]

Wow! Dr. Cho's testimony certainly drives home the power of using your imagination in partnership with God. However, found within his testimony is a very important element: intentionality. Dr. Cho did not sit at home and wait for God to bring one million people before he would preach. He was intentional in his plan. He preached for three years before he saw his dream for three-hundred come true, and then he dreamed a bigger dream. He continued to expand his dream until he felt fulfilled, but God was not finished! God had a dream even bigger than Dr. Cho's. He started his dreaming with the ability to imagine three hundred, while in reality God's dream was of reaching over one million.

When you begin to dream with God in specific details, He begins to create the answer for you. He starts to work toward the fulfillment of your dream, because He loves to fill the desires of your heart. So, it is critical for you to discover what passions God has placed in your heart. What do you burn so deeply for you cannot imagine your life without it? Once you have uncovered some dreams you would like realized in your life, then the work begins.

I have spent many hours dreaming with God and dreaming BIG! One of the dreams began with a simple conversation with God. I said to the Lord, "I would love to write books that would bring people closer to you the way other books have for me." That is when the ideas began flowing without me even realizing

---

2 Friedel, Dewey, *Imagine THAT!* (Shippensburg: Destiny Image Publishers Inc., 2006), Kindle 560

it was the path to publication. It was a day or two before the New Year and I was praying about my New Year's resolution. The Lord began speaking to me about writing a blog each week for my New Year Resolution. Nervously, I said yes! I began writing a blog every week for one year under the title "Believing God and Believing His Word." I stayed the course; I was diligent, obedient and faithful! After the first year God had me continue the blog for several more years. God has blown me away with His fulfillment.

Let me tell you what I do with my dreams. I have giant post-it notes on the wall in my office. Listed are my dreams; I read through them, declare them and talk to Poppa-God about them.

Here are just a few of the things God and I have and continue to dream about:

- I dream about my children, and generations to follow, loving God. God had shown me through His promise to my mother that this would come to pass.

- I dreamed about earning my degree, and God had me start a Bible college in our Apostolic Center where I earned my doctorate.

- I dream of traveling and helping people encounter God. God has taken me to Haiti, Colombia, Taiwan, Africa, and Nicaragua as well as many cities in the US.

- I dream of miracles, signs and wonders released continuously.

- I dream of having worship so pure it provokes the heart of God to show up in a tangible way.

I want you to DREAM and DREAM BIG! As you can see, some of my dreams have been answered, some are just getting started, and some are still waiting to be realized. Regardless of the circumstances, I did not give up on my dreams with God.

I have learned when I start to strive and stress for an outcome, that it then it becomes frustratingly hard and at times discouraging. If I step back and focus my attention on our relationship and rest in Him, everything begins to flow. In other words, my striving creates delay and my trusting God speeds up the process!

This has become one of my favorite Scriptures:

"It was like a dream come true when You freed us from captivity and brought us back to Zion. We laughed and laughed, and overflowed with gladness! We were left shouting with joy and singing Your praise. All the nations saw it and joined in, saying, "The Lord has done great miracles for them!" Yes, He did mighty miracles and we are overjoyed! Now Lord, do it again!" (Psalm 126:1-4 TPT)

Who Is Standing with You?

We need each other to accomplish our dreams. For me, my husband has been the greatest cheerleader. He has encouraged me and made a place for my dreams in our marriage. His favorite quote is by Napoleon Hill, "Whatever the mind can conceive and believe, it can achieve," and he lives it every day! In addition, I have my long-time three best friends who are like sisters. These are the ones who stand with me.

In the Bible, God shows us the power of relationship: Abraham and Sarah, Jonathan and David, Elijah and Elisha, Joseph and Mary, and John and Peter are only a few. In each relationship, they stood beside each other encouraging, serving, and protecting the other in marriage, in friendship and in family.

Do you have these people in your life? Ones with whom you can be transparent? Ones who will pray for you? Ones who love you unconditionally? If your answer is yes, treasure the richness of your relationship. If no, ask God to bring these relationships into your life. I cannot stress how important it is to be in right relationships in realizing your dreams. We are designed to need each other! "A dear friend will love you no matter what, and a family sticks together through all kinds of trouble" (Proverbs 17:17 TPT).

What Can You Believe For?

We will always have opposition to our dreams. "A thief has only one thing in mind: he wants to steal, kill, and destroy" (John 10:10 TPT). He wants to steal your hopes and dreams to get you to stop short of God's plans. We cannot lose heart and allow the enemy's plan to destroy or overtake us. We have to keep our eyes focused on God and His ability to intervene on our behalf.

King David was one of the greatest examples of pressing through all the challenges until his dream, his promise, was fulfilled. His relationship with God in the beginning defined him as a worshipper. Later on, he received a promise to be king. First, though, he had to become a warrior, defending Israel and fighting to stay one step ahead of his enemy, King Saul. David had his ups and downs in physical battles and emotional discouragement, but he knew the end goal. He was to be crowned King of Israel; it was the dream God planned for him.

These are King David's words,

"I would have lost heart, unless I had believed that I would see the goodness of the Lord in the land of the living. Wait on the Lord; be of good courage, and He shall strengthen your heart; Wait, I say, on the Lord!" (Psalm 27:13-14 NKJV)

Here is a testimony of the Lord bringing freedom from the enemy's attempt at destruction in Kathryn's life.

It is interesting how every time my husband goes out of town, the Lord brings healing to me, so I can become closer to Him. The first time my husband went away on a mission trip, the Lord took me back through every fear I ever had in my life. And I was delivered from a spirit of fear.

More recently, He cleansed the cellular memory in my body of consternation.

Consternation is a sudden, alarming amazement or dread that can cause one to become completely befuddled. In my case, it was as if all my thoughts had been strewn about and nothing made sense.

So, my mind knew the truth of the situation, but my body reacted irrationally, and my mind eventually became undone. An example is when I walked through a dark room. In my mind, I knew no one was there, but from past experiences of being grabbed in the dark, my body would become anxious and my pulse would quicken while my stomach churned in a fight or flight response. No matter how much I self-talked and prayed, I could not get my body to have peace. While praying and spending time with

God, He taught me that my cells carried the past memories of trauma and that I needed to pray and cleanse them, so they could begin to react in a normal way. I prayed and cleansed my body with the Word and the Blood of Jesus, thanking my cells for protecting me, but acknowledging that Jesus had me now and they didn't need to respond in such a way any longer. I am finally healed.

It is still curious to go through the same actions that normally brought fear to my body, and now no longer experience a reaction at all. It was also during this time that God reminded me of a word of knowledge I had received from a well-known minister and prophet. He called me over to him at a conference and said, "You have had nightmares and night-terrors since you were a child, haven't you?" My reply was, "Yes, I had night terrors until I was in my 30s and my dreams are always scary." His reply was one I did not expect as he explained the enemy had tried to scare me so I would be afraid of everything and not be able to walk in my anointing. My anointing is that of an oracle of God. I was shocked. It made so much sense as to why I had so much difficulty expressing myself.

A few months later, my husband went on another trip, and once again, God began to move. Curiously, God led me to a video which had just been released the day before. It was about a leader of a church and his experience with crippling anxiety. The next day, I experienced anxiety like I had never experienced before. Years ago, I'd struggled with anxiety, and God had healed me of it along with panic attacks, but now it was back, even worse. I called my pastor and we did a SOZO, a time of emotional healing prayer, over the phone, and I received a good deal of relief. Later that night, one of my prayer partners dropped by my house as God directed her. As we prayed, God revealed that I had been repressing my feelings since I was a young child. I had never felt safe to express my true feelings, so I just locked them away.

However, God was saying it was time to learn to be vulnerable and experience my emotions. That is truly difficult for someone with a history of abuse; the only feelings I could identify were fear and anger. God explained that as I felt an emotion rising up, I was to experience and identify it and then give it to Him. As I followed the process, I soon realized there were many feelings I had to rely on the Holy Spirit to identify so I could complete the process. It actually became fun to identify my feelings and give them to God to be redeemed. Allowing myself to be vulnerable and authentic would bring me into freedom I had never experienced. It also released a new joy in my life, and I have been told I am more jovial. Although my anointing as an oracle is not yet fully realized, I know God will continue to work in me to bring it to fullness. – *Kathryn*

"Whatever God has promised gets stamped with the yes of Jesus. In Him, this is what we preach and pray, the great Amen, God's yes and our yes together, gloriously evident. God affirms us, making us a sure thing in Christ, putting his yes within us. By his Spirit, he has stamped us with his eternal pledge--a sure beginning of what he is destined to complete" (1 Corinthians 1:20 MSG).

Dream Big Dreams;
I Will Fulfill Them for You....
Abba

Digging Deeper

- Set aside some time to dream, and dream big with God.

- Invite Him to open up the realm of possibilities and start making a list of all the things you hunger to see come to life!

- Imagine what it would look like to have your dreams come to life.

- Do not worry about your dreams being holy enough; seek God, and His dreams will refine yours. Remember, the Spirit of the Living God dwells in us.

- Do not tell God how to fulfill your dream. I am not saying to not be specific in your dreams. What I am saying is do not try to manage the end result God has planned for you. His fulfillment is abundantly, exceedingly more than you can imagine!

- Do not give up. Your dreams may happen this afternoon while you are making dinner or on Monday morning as you get ready for the work.

Chapter 2

THE LONGING OF OUR HEART

"When Christians say the Christ-life is in them, they do not mean simply something mental or moral. When they speak of being 'in Christ' or of Christ being 'in them,' this is not simply a way of saying that they are thinking about Christ or copying Him. They mean that Christ is actually operating through them..." —C. S. Lewis[3]

---

3 Lewis, C.S., *Mere Christianity*. (London: Macmillan Publishers, 1978), 64,65.

The words of C.S. Lewis cited on the previous page describe with exactness the longing of my heart for the reality of Christ in me. It all began when I was nine years old when I said yes to Jesus. I remember the day like it was yesterday. It was a typical hot summer day in Chattanooga, Tennessee. My grandparents, Luke and Gladys – Papa and Granny to me – had dropped me off for a five-day camp. They sent each of their grandchildren annually to camp once they reached nine years old. Typically, I was very outgoing and friendly, but it was the first time I had gone away without my older siblings, Kathy, Becky and Mark. I was nervous and unsure about spending the week with a bunch of strangers.

Forever clearly etched in my memory were three events I experienced at camp. Two of them were traumatizing to my awkward pre-adolescent age. The last event set me on a twenty-something-year journey searching for Jesus, or as Lewis wrote, for Christ "actually operating through" me.

My first day of camp we went swimming, and this would set the tone for the rest of the week. All the girls went first, then the boys. Did I mention it was a Baptist camp? No "mixed swimming" was allowed! Of course, being from Georgia and spending many weekends at Lake Allatoona, I could swim—that wasn't the problem. The real challenge was my fair skin. Sunscreen was not available! I had to always wear my dad's oversized, white t-shirt to protect as much of my skin as possible. But there was nothing for my face and my arms, and they were burnt to a crisp that very first day. I spent the rest of the week with a bright red face and half-white, half-red arms – and no momma to nurse my painfully, blistered skin.

My next adventure was not as physically painful but equally as traumatizing. As I think about the details, I am quickly transported back in time with the smell of horses and swarming flies. The heat was sweltering, and it was my first time riding. We all lined up in front of our assigned horse. My horse was brown with a white streak between his eyes; I believe his name was Brownie. His stature was daunting next to my sunburned, nine-year-old frame. The counselors had to put a step stool next to my horse, so I could reach my foot in the stirrup as they helped me pull myself up by the horn onto the battered saddle. Steadying myself in the saddle, we headed down a green, grassy hill toward the trail. As Brownie took his first steps, terror ran though my insides, even though I smiled and pretended everything was perfect. Suddenly, he began to trot! To me it seemed like the gates had just opened at the Kentucky Derby and I found myself hanging on for dear life as we headed down the hill. No sooner had I adjusted to his trot than I saw we were aiming straight for a sprawling oak tree. I grasped the reins even tighter! The limbs of the oak seemed to expand like a spider's web planning for my capture. In a split second, I panicked. I JUMPED OFF the horse! I did not get hurt, though the counselors were not very happy with me. My horseback riding days ended not only for the week, but also pretty much for the rest of my life!

The last day was the end of my camp experience, but it gave me a life-altering unexpected encounter with Jesus. I was happy to be going home and the chapel was my final hurdle. Our group entered the hot, musty, small chapel, finding our seats on the long, dark wooden benches. As chapel began, something felt different; there was a stirring inside of me. I was listening to the preacher speak on how we could invite Jesus to live in our hearts, when suddenly the sound of his voice became distant and muffled... the Presence of Jesus overwhelmed me. I began to shake and cry. Faintly, I heard the preacher invite everyone who wanted to ask Jesus into his or her heart to come forward. Sliding out to the end of the bench, I stepped into the aisle with all intentions of going to the front. Instead, I found myself leaning with my back against the wall. It was as if my shoulders and hands had become glued there. I trembled all over as I felt His Presence.

I did not understand what had happened. Something was different. Something had changed in me. Jesus became real and tangible to my nine-year-old heart. My newly discovered encounter with Jesus should have been a day of celebration. However, it ended up being a secret between Jesus and me after I left camp that day to go home. You see, when our bus arrived at my grandparents' church we had the closing ceremonies in the sanctuary. It was there that Dr. Lee Roberts announced the sudden loss of a pillar in the church, Lucian R. Jernigan, who had passed on to glory. I looked at the girl next to me and said, "That's my grandfather's name, too." I did not realize it was my beloved papa, until my other grandfather came to pick me up. My parents were not believers and my grandmother was lost in her grief, so I never did get the opportunity to talk about what happened in the chapel that day.

From that day forward, it was just Jesus and me… and I wanted to get to know Him more.

My First Inkling of More

I knew one verse in the Bible: John 3:16, "For God so loved the world, that he gave his only begotten Son, that whosoever believeth in him should not perish, but have everlasting life" (KJV). This verse became my TRUMP CARD! I pulled it out in times of distress, especially when I needed hope and comfort – like when I would spend time at my granny's farm in the summer. She would pray with me at bedtime and ask God to keep Satan from snatching me away in the middle night. Hiding under my blankets, I would recite John 3:16. I felt safe; He was there with me. My understanding was so limited, except I knew repeating the Scripture and just saying His name out loud, over and over, made me aware He was with me. He was in my heart. He was protecting me.

Six years would pass before I had my first inkling that there was more to Jesus. It came in a surprise encounter at my best friend's youth group. There was a small group of teens visiting her youth group and sharing about the love of Jesus. They were cool, with their bell-bottom jeans and fringed vests. We were never allowed to wear jeans to our church! They had a guitar and sat on the floor singing and talking with us. I remember I said a cuss word. I quickly apologized, mumbling something about trying to do better. One of the girls looked at me, without even acknowledging my words, and poured out the love of Jesus through her words. I had never experienced anything like this.

In that moment of time, I realized there was more to Jesus than calling out His name and reciting John 3:16. My hunger was rekindled for the Jesus I had experienced at camp. I just wanted more, and frankly, I did not know how to get more. I spent the next decade in and out of churches, looking for His more.

My first real attempt at the church thing began in Louisiana. My daughter, Katie, was three months old and my son, Ross, was two years old. My husband and I were attending a local church when we decided to have our children baptized. We were assigned an elder to mentor us in the membership requirements in order for the baptism to occur. There were so many hoops for us to jump through, and it soon became obvious that conformity was their baseline. It was conformity to the denomination and conformity was familiar. So, I conformed, just as my family always did during our occasional church visit when I was a child.

Got my hat and my gloves: check
Sunday School first, followed by three hymns and a sermon: check
Volunteering: check

I learned more about Jesus during our time there while enjoying new friends, potluck dinners, children's Christmas plays and the Minnie Mouse Easter egg hunts. Nevertheless, I was still missing the tangible, realness of Jesus. His tangible Presence was not there, at least, not for me. I knew there was more, but the more I came for was definitely not there. My search would continue as I looked for the more of Jesus I was longing after.

Our family moved several more times and with this, we experienced three more churches, but none of them touched what

Jesus had stirred in me. Yet with each one, I could sense a deeper awareness of Jesus coaxing me closer. He was drawing me in to search for Him, to move beyond John 3:16, and to move into the reality of His love for me.

He was extending an invitation for intimacy and it was working! My awareness of His great love for me exploded as this wondrous intimacy between Him and me grew. I seemed to be able to sense His Presence with me, while still not grasping the truth of His Presence living in me.

One of the things that came to light was my understanding of John 3:16. At the time I was mostly focused on how Jesus's death on the cross brought forgiveness of my sins, giving me eternal life. It was all about making it to Heaven. Somehow, I missed the reason for Jesus's death on the cross: His love. His love for you and His love for me! We are LOVED by Him! Jesus gave His life so we could be loved where we are now, not just when we get into Heaven. An awakening to His INTIMATE LOVE began to explode in me. I began to find myself wondering, "Why does He love me?" My quest for experiencing His love became an insatiable passion.

I began to make my list of things to talk with Him about in prayer. Just this little move toward Him began to grow my awareness of a new closeness with Him. At times, I felt we were a team. I was learning to consult with Jesus, like I did with my husband Chuck as my partner. This was all new to me! I was testing and trying different approaches. I really just wanted to know:

Who are You, Jesus?

Why do You love me?

What do You want from me?

How do I live with You in my life?

Then Suddenly — Answers

I include an epilogue, "My Journey with Jesus," at the end of my books. It shares a more detailed account of my journey. This little snippet below highlights the turning point for me. It came through a crisis in my life that was painful; except Jesus used it to dramatically change my relationship with Him forever. As my relationship with Him grew, all my questions slowly began to be answered through His love and His passion for me.

My best friend, my confidante, the woman who loved me unconditionally, my mom, died at the young age of fifty-nine. To this day, I cherish and love her deeply. Mom had her encounter with Jesus before she turned fifty and through that she became a great person of prayer. She spent the last six years of her life living and traveling with us and enjoying her grandchildren. Her relationship with Jesus greatly influenced our lives. With her loss, my search intensified. I was desperate to find the truth about God.

So, I challenged God to prove Himself. I gave Him goals and deadlines. Being a corporate executive, that was the framework I lived in, and it was what I knew. So, I gave God timeframes, objectives and outcomes He had to meet. He had one year to show up, or I was going to give up! He had to teach me about all this stuff or I was going to quit believing, because in my heart, there was no other option. Even as I write this, I shudder at what could have been interpreted by others as arrogance or even ridiculousness, when in reality, it was my desperation for more crying out for the Living Christ whom I had encountered. The timeframe I gave Him was one year. The goal I expected Him to meet was to teach me about Him. The outcome was I would know He was real—as real as I had experienced when I was nine years old. I told Him I would do my part, which honestly, in the beginning was more formulaic than heartfelt. I committed to spending at least five minutes each day with Him, and I had a prayer list that I would review with Him regularly. A perfect business deal, right?

But what happened next was extra-ordinary. God was so faithful to me, as He responded to my passionate pleas. He began to flood me with His Presence – tangible Presence! I could feel Him, I could see Him in visions, and I could hear His voice. It was as if all my senses were opened, including taste and aromas. Trances and insights, prophetic visions and words of knowledge—I was completely undone with His holiness. I had no idea how to define this in the confines of the church. I had never heard of anything like this. Of course, in hindsight, these were found all though Scripture, I had just never read them.

As I experienced this new revelation of who He is, I realized this was just a glimpse of the incredible beauty, the magnificent splendor of Jesus coming alive in me! He came alive in me – I could see Him. He showed up in the most unexpected places, and He surprised me all the time. He was real and tangible, mysterious and full of wonder. Whew – I was overwhelmed!

Suddenly, my life was turned upside down. I was hungry to read the Word like never before. As I read, it was like a movie playing through my mind, capturing each word in living color. God began surprising me in a tangible, real, fragrant encounter with Him by opening all my senses to His Presence! Honestly, after all the years of longing, it was a little overwhelming.

One encounter made an indelible mark on me, ingrained forever. As I recall it today, it is as fresh as it was the day it happened. There was nothing out of the ordinary about that day. I had been spending most mornings at the park after my children left for school. I would bring my Bible, journal and a hot cup of coffee and spend time talking to the Lord. This morning was no different. I sat on top of the picnic table overlooking the lake, and what happened next completely unraveled me. A movie began to play in front of me, which I learned later was a trance as in Acts 10:10. As I watched, I saw Jesus facing me with His hands on my shoulders. He said, "I am with you; you are walking with Me." Then the Father was to my right with the Holy Spirit behind me, leaning over my left shoulder smiling. Jesus and the Father were in a formed presence while the Holy Spirit was more transparent, with less form, yet vibrant. In the vision, they were encircling me. I closed my eyes, to see if this was real and I could still see Them. When I opened my eyes, They were still there. The trance did

The Beauty of Journaling

As I review my journal from that encounter many years ago, I am immediately drawn back again into these experiences. They are alive in me, because Jesus is alive in me. These encounters are part of my DNA; they cannot be erased. The life they carry gives me the access to experience the tenderness over and over again. They are forever available, always alive, and fully accessible. When you journal, God will do the same for you. There is power in capturing every moment with God. For each moment is infused with life, connecting you deeper into the oneness of God and giving you immediate access through the reliving of these encounters.

not last long; however, it was a line of demarcation for me as I felt the physicality of Their Presence as Father, Son and Holy Spirit. After the trance ended, I began to sketch the vision in my journal, realizing in that moment we were joined as one. I wrote in big bold letters on the page JOINED AS ONE. This one experience sparked something inside of me to know and to come to understand the fullness of being JOINED AS ONE with the Father, Son and Holy Spirit.

JOINED AS ONE

Over the years of studying the Scriptures, one book, the Book of John, captured my heart. I loved his poetic writing and relational conversations with Jesus. I was especially fond of the way he described himself, *as the one Jesus loved.* I wanted to be the one Jesus loved, just like John. It wasn't that I wanted Jesus to love me more than anyone else; I just wanted to know in a deep-seated way, in my bones and in every fiber of my body, that He loved me.

I especially loved reading chapters 13-17 over and over again. The first time I read the words, I was captured by the intimate exchange between Jesus and His disciples. He gathers them in the Upper Room to prepare them for what is to come, and He speaks to them face to face, as friends.

Each time I read this section, His words transport me back in time. Suddenly, a vision in my mind takes me to the Upper Room where I would join Him and the disciples at the table.

The room feels small with each disciple tightly wedged-in together. Glancing around, I see a towel and a basin of water, now murky with the dirt from Jesus washing each of the His disciples' feet. On the table are half-empty cups with a little food scattered about from supper.

I observe as Jesus leans in and begins to speak. John, sitting next Him, turns his full attention to Jesus, as Peter moves in closer to grasp every spoken word. I take a moment to capture the emotion of the room; all eyes are locked on Jesus with intensity. Jesus leans in further; the disciples mirror His action. He begins to release a prophetic picture of what is to come. He is conveying with exactness though they cannot comprehend what He is saying. No stone is left unturned. He is telling them exactly what to expect as His death is nearing. I am sensing the tension in the air.

Now I find myself leaning in as He breathes this fresh new revelation. He tells us He is leaving and going to be with the Father, but we will not be left alone. No, because They, He and the Father, have a plan! Clinging to every spoken word, there is anticipation of the unveiling of the plan. Then, I hear Jesus say in the most assuring voice, "I am in the Father, and the Father in Me, and when I am reunited with Him, He and I will live in each of you." As the last word leaves His lips, there is an audible gasp in the air. He continues, "This is Our plan for your future, so you will never be separated from Us. This is the way you will live in this world, completely connected to Us. Us in you is the greater truth you will live from."

My mind screams, "What! What?" The magnitude of His words is too much to comprehend, too much to absorb! And then my spirit softly whispers, "Yes." Every fiber of my being tingles with excitement as this resonates in me, because when I was nine years old, the Jesus I encountered then, was the Jesus I was encountering now.

These unexpected words of oneness suddenly apprehend me. Finally, I have a glimmer of what I have been searching for, and it goes way beyond what I expected. Until I first had this experience, my understanding had been limited to the presumed symbolic gesture of accepting Christ into my heart, and now it was replaced with the TRUTH of Christ, literally living in me!

CHRIST LIVING IN ME!

CHRIST LIVING IN ME!

CHRIST LIVING IN ME!

I turned to Jesus with my mind echoing "What?" and my spirit saying, "Yes!" I asked Him what has now become my favorite question, "Jesus, how does this work?"

How do I live in this world moment by moment knowing YOU are living in me?

Collecting Treasures

It is funny when we ask God about stuff; He likes to answer us in very unique ways. I personally would prefer His answers to come in audible instructions or by email with a step-by-step plan or even on an app for our phone. Except, God in all His grandeur has created a much better mechanism: ONENESS WITH HIM. Oneness involves a well-thought-out collection of treasures that unfold in our daily lives.

The greatest treasure I have found is Jesus. I soon began to discover other treasures for my collection. Like the one I discovered from John: Christ is in me. These treasures are like jewels – flawless diamonds: beautifully clear and without blemish. Another treasure I discovered was that I was His treasure too.

God began to answer my How questions by pushing me out of my comfort zone. Little by little, He began nudging me to share my journey of discovering His oneness. With much trepidation I shared with my friends, then in groups and finally, by writing about my encounters with Him. It was definitely a little scary. I felt like I wasn't educated enough in the Word, and I didn't know Him enough to share these kinds of things. During this time, my pastor, Dr. Peyton Johnson, was instrumental in helping connect what God was showing me with the truth in His Word. The more I shared, the more I learned.

Next, He asked me to write a book about all the treasures I had discovered about our oneness. I was overwhelmed and excited at the same time. I said, "YES Lord!" I remember telling the Lord, "I am committing my time to writing about the truth of Your Word, what we experienced together, and the testimonies of others, so others can find the treasure of oneness in You."

What else could I have said? But in the back of my head, there was a little voice saying, "Really, God? I am so busy already!" I could not imagine devoting more time to writing. My first book, *Believing God and Believing His Word*, was still in pre-release and I was finalizing the edits on my second book, *7 Visions: A Glimpse of the Father's Heart*. Plus, I was completing my doctorate, teaching at another school, acting as the Senior Leader at our Gathering Apostolic Center and Senior Pastor at the Gathering with Jesus. Did I mention I had a family, too?

Then, there is God. Nothing else matters; He works it all out. I can meander, whine, and debate, but then there is God, and when He moves, everything falls into place. Regardless of my schedule, the fact remained: GOD WAS COMMISSIONING ME TO WRITE!

With my Yes, the words began to play like a movie in my mind and then flowed onto the pages. At other times, He began to download new thoughts and insights that would consume me all night and all day long. I would awaken with sentences already formed in my mind, and I knew they were not mine! He did not wait until I was ready to receive, sitting at the computer, Bible open and coffee poured. No! Pictures, words, and new concepts would come at any given moment while driving or cooking dinner or even while taking a shower, which was the most awkward. I would find myself writing keywords on the steam-covered glass and then trying to capture them before they melted away. I would run to my computer to write what He was telling me, though my typing was nowhere near the speed of the flow of His words. And just when I thought we were finished, He would begin again. He would lean in, closing the space between us, so I could go deeper.

I had to be on *high alert* and prepared at all times, or I would find myself scrambling for something to write on. Early mornings seemed to be the best for me, except His words and thoughts were not confined to my best times. As He spoke, I wrote, and then I would read and re-read my written words and be completely amazed.

On one occasion I was working on a homework assignment, which was to read Ephesians 1:3,

"Everything heaven contains has already been lavished upon us as a live gift from our wonderful heavenly Father, the Father of our Lord Jesus – all because He sees us in Christ." (TPT)

All of a sudden, the words "in Christ" echoed in me, "in Christ, in Christ." This is what the Holy Spirit began to unfold as I wrote in my journal:

Abba, You see me in Christ... in Christ... in Christ...

Abba, Christ is in me and I am in Christ; this is my connection.

I want you to also fully experience the revelation I had at that moment:

- Stop and close your eyes for a moment and allow this truth to sink deep down inside.

  When the eyes of the Father are looking at you, He sees you through Christ—the you He created you to be.

- Allow your imagination to fully grasp what is being said here.

- Now, go look into a mirror, and say, "I see what the Father sees: I see me in Jesus."

Is This New for You?

For me, when God began to reveal this layer of understanding, I began to jump up and down with excitement! The words of the Holy Spirit reverberated through me: Christ in me. The way the Father sees me is in Christ. Immediately, He brought me back to one of my favorite Scriptures. I have mulled over and studied for years:

"...that they all may be one, as You, Father, are in Me, and I in You; that they also may be one in Us, that the world may believe that You sent Me" (John 17:21 NKJV).

"The Father is in Christ, Christ is in the Father and They are in me," flooded my mind. They are not separate from each other or from me; I am joined with them by the Holy Spirit. This is the greater truth I was learning to draw from, a truth, a continuing revelation, for me to live from.

Then these questions started coming to me...

- Lord, what does this look like in each day of my life?

- How do I live out of the fullness of You living in me?

This is not unusual for me; my chatter with God is filled with many questions and ensuing discussions, which have always pushed me into a deeper relationship with Him. I do not want to have intellectual knowledge of Him, but knowledge birthed from an intimacy of conversation and time spent together.

Like John the Apostle, I want to be close enough to lay my head on His chest. For some of you, there has been a time when you have felt the tangible encounter with Jesus and you have leaned back to rest on Him. For others, this may be foreign, unattainable, and too hard to imagine or comprehend. This may not fit your theology, it may be beyond your experience, but don't give up.

Trust the process and let's go through it together. You will develop the closeness to rest your head on His chest.

Each chapter will end with a **Digging Deeper** section. I challenge you to dig in to this journey of taking your relationship with God deeper. It will only happen by spending time with Him, studying with Him and wrestling with those ideas that are new to you. As the Holy Spirit teaches you, don't forget to journal everything. Writing it down brings clarity and records your journey.

Digging Deeper:

1. **Pray:**

   Jesus, as I go on this journey of oneness with You, I ask you to open my understanding. Draw me close and show me how to live my life in oneness with You. Thank You, Jesus. Amen

2. **Read John 17:**

   Now focus your attention on verse 21 reading the words aloud:

   "…that they all may be one, as You, Father, are in Me, and I in You; that they also may be one in Us, that the world may believe that You sent Me" (John 17:21 NKJV).

   • Write down your thoughts about the words Jesus is speaking to the Father.

   • What do these words mean to you?

3. **Read Ephesians 1:3 aloud:**

   "Everything heaven contains has already been lavished upon us as a live gift from our wonderful heavenly Father, the Father of our Lord Jesus – all because He sees us in Christ" (TPT).

   • Ask the Lord to give you words and pictures to describe how He sees you.

- Write down everything He is sharing with you.

God wants to give you fresh revelation of His Oneness with you. He wants you to know what your life in Him looks like every day. He wants to teach you how to live in the abundant life He has planned for you. **God wants to give you MORE!**

Chapter 3

Did You RSVP?

"What is life but God's daring invitation to embark on a remarkable journey?"[4]

— Craig D. Lounsbrough

---

4 Lonsbrough,Craig D., *An Intimate Collision: Encounters with Life and Jesus,* https://www.goodreads.com/quotes/tag/invitation, (accessed 08/03/2017).

Whem Jesus walked on earth, His message went viral! He invited everyone to follow Him. His invitation was inclusive; everyone was invited to encounter the love of the Father through Him. He had the best social media available: word of mouth!

Everyone everywhere was talking about Him. Men, women and children were trying to comprehend what was really happening right before their very eyes. They not only heard His words, which at times were outrageous; they watched Him do unprecedented and completely unpredictable miracles.

Like the time He turned water into wine; only it wasn't just any wine – it was the best wine they had ever had! It made no sense – but Jesus did it anyway!

For you and me, Jesus's action is beyond our understanding. However, for the people at the wedding, it was an invitation to encounter God's best. Only a few would have seen Jesus perform the actual miracle, even so, all of the guests were fortunate recipients of the best wine Heaven had to offer!

Invitation for Truth

One morning, as I was worshiping, I felt a whisper from the Lord to look at His invitation to Nicodemus, found in John 3:1-21. Nicodemus was an influential and respected member of the highest religious council, the Sanhedrin, who were embroiled in heated arguments against Jesus. This Council had dedicated their lives to the Law of Moses, and now Jesus seemed to be threatening those very laws, stirring up fear and anger among them.

Nicodemus sought out Jesus in the dark of night because his spirit had been stirred and he had to know who Jesus really was. Picture that night in your mind.

The moon and stars are the only illumination, as Nicodemus slips out of his familiar surroundings. Finding Jesus alone, away from His small band of followers, Nicodemus approaches Him. He opens the conversation with a statement of affirmation, "You are a teacher from God, for no one performs the miraculous signs that You do, unless God's power is with him" (John 3:2 TPT).

Have you ever noticed Jesus rarely responds to what the person has said? Listen to Jesus's response to Nicodemus's acknowledgement that He is a teacher from God.

> "Jesus answered and said to him, 'Most assuredly, I say to you, unless one is born again, he cannot see the kingdom of God'" (John 3:3 NKJV).

These words leave Nicodemus stunned! Nicodemus is looking for Jesus to affirm and elaborate on his statement that He is a teacher from God. Instead, Jesus makes a radical statement, which contains more than Nicodemus can comprehend. Nicodemus cannot grasp Jesus's words "to be born again," let alone the concept of being able to see the Kingdom. You can almost feel his whole body shake involuntarily. Was this truth? Was this blasphemy? He had spent his whole life studying and understanding the signs, so he could recognize the Messiah—the bodily presence of

God sent from Heaven. And now it was happening; his dream was coming true. But, it came in unfamiliar words from someone who did not have the pedigree Nicodemus had, nor was Jesus part of the priestly system set up by the law. Nicodemus's mind was paralyzed and his ears closed.

Can you imagine the thoughts that exploded in his mind? In silence, he mentally scanned the scrolls he had memorized and studied since he was a young boy. Then he fast-forwarded through Genesis to Isaiah to Jeremiah, trying to connect, trying to understand, trying to make sense of the words born-again, seeing the kingdom. Nicodemus was looking for truth from his knowledge stored in his mind.

Listen to the words I heard Dr. Brian Simmons speak at the Women on the Frontline conference in Phoenix. I was taught and then I even taught it myself that the longest journey to Christ is the eighteen inches connecting our head to our heart. With Jesus's words, Nicodemus was trying to take what was stuck in his head, his intellect, down eighteen inches to his heart! It was impossible because Nicodemus, like I did, had the direction of the eighteen inches reversed. Dr. Simmons explained the correct process beautifully.

Truth cannot come into the mind; it has to come
into the spirit.
The door to truth is not intellect.
The door to truth is the spirit yielded to God.
If it is not in your heart, it is not real.
It goes from the heart to the head.[5]

5 Dr. Brian Simmons' Message, Women on the Frontlines (WOFL) 2017 World Convention, – Phoenix, AZ

Nicodemus was trying to RSVP to a truth from his knowledge. Jesus was inviting him to RSVP from his spirit to God in order to be able to receive these truths. Nicodemus's only response was:

"How can a man be born when he is old? Can he enter a second time into his mother's womb and be born?" (John 3:4 NKJV)

Think about this: Nicodemus's meeting with Jesus released the core revelation that could change his life and the lives of the Jewish people forever. Their conversation was an invitation to Nicodemus to be the religious leader who confirmed Jesus as their long-awaited Messiah. As a teacher, Nicodemus had prepared his entire life to recognize the Messiah. Now Jesus was revealing a truth to Nicodemus no one else had yet heard. Nicodemus wrestled to move outside the constructs of his knowledge into a move of his spirit.

Can you identify with his struggle? I know I have wrestled with my knowledge on many occasions, wanting to have a familiar answer from God. Instead, these have been His invitation to me to learn a new thought process for my life.

Let me share with you a testimony of how God invited me in to receive in my spirit. a truth about who He is. I awoke one morning a few years back to the Father's voice revealing who He is in the form of "I AM" statements. To my surprise, it was not just a one-time occurrence. Every day for over a month, He shared a total of 44 "I AM" statements with me. Some days, He would elaborate on two or three names. Many of the names were familiar: "I am your Father who loves you." Others I wrestled with: "I am Your Father who will provide all that you need and over and above all that need – abundance!"

Having a Father who would provide was a little hard for me to grasp. I knew in my mind it was biblical, but it was not in my spirit, so it was not yet real as my truth. At the time, my business was failing due to the downturn in the housing market. The business had accumulated debt and sales were flat. My general manager had moved and with my other responsibilities, I could not run it by myself. My plan was to sell the business and pay off the debt. However, my plan was not working! I began to feel that the Lord wanted me to simply close the business. It didn't make any sense. I asked the Lord over and over, "How can I do that with all the debt I have?" I even received prophetic words from others about closing my business, and the words would make me mad! I was scared to RSVP to Jesus's invitation to trust that His Father would supply everything I needed.

My husband and I stepped up our prayers and reached out to others for prayer. The time came when I knew the Lord was saying, "Now," but nothing had changed. I still had all the debt. The thought of closing the business with debt made no economic sense. But, I was obedient to His direction and I closed it! Immediately, my husband's business increased in sales and profits and we were able to pay off all the debt within months. Over $130,000 in debt was paid off by the Father who supplied over and above all that I needed…abundance!

His truth moved to my heart and became real in my life!

I still read over these "I AM" statements, slowly allowing them to become truth in my heart so I can use them with my mind. I am learning how to hear the Father's voice and lean into what He is saying. I am learning a whole new understanding of my identity in Him and to give room to His voice to speak. I am learning to

RSVP to His invitation to show up and spend time in the secret place where we can talk for hours. This has been a wonderful birthing of intimacy for me each time we meet together.

Like Nicodemus, you are invited to receive spirit revelation, which at times goes against your knowledge and your culture. If you are not willing to receive it, you will not be able to move forward. For all of us it is so much easier to stay with the familiar. However, the familiar can obstruct the sound of His beckoning. His sound draws you into a journey He has intricately planned for you! His invitation will awaken your senses to a new life in His Presence.

Every Minute Counts!

Now, when Photini encountered Jesus, she ran as fast as she could, not wasting a minute to share the revelation He gave her. Who is she, you ask? Her story is found in John 4. Mostly she is known as the Samaritan, the woman at the well. Recently, I gained a new perspective on Photini's life from Dr. Brian Simmons, as he shared some insights he had gained while translating the Bible into his series, *The Passion Translation*. (If you have never read this new version of the Bible, don't wait any longer. It is amazing!)[6]

Sometimes, the completion of someone life, like Photini's, isn't documented in the Bible, so I was excited to see where the journey took her, once she said YES to Jesus's invitation. And I love her story! There are a couple specific things that captured my heart about her that I am excited to share with you. I know she will inspire as you discover the rest of her story!

---

6 *The Passion Translation*, (Copyright © 2017 by BroadStreet Publishing® Group, LLC) is a version of the Psalms, Proverbs, Song of Solomon and the New Testament by Brian Simmons. The complete translation is available both as a Bible style collection (TPT) or as individual books.

Photini had lost her identity. Her sordid past had defined her, and her entire town viewed her through these errors in her judgment. These words were descriptive of her identity based on what she did, not on who she was created to be:

Rejected by men

Shunned by others

Shamed by too many marriages

Failure as a woman

Her soul was hurting. She had to be intentional in planning every outing down to gathering water, so no one would be around to stare, to whisper about her and to mock her. She couldn't face any more public humiliation.

Have you ever been through a time when your identity was defined by a mistake? Where you avoided going places, because you just could not take the judgment in the eyes of the people who would be there? It is so painful to be trapped by the past. Photini knew this pain. She was trapped with seemingly no way out.

When Photini met Jesus, she had nothing to lose, so she questioned Him. And with each question, each challenge raised by His response, Photini's old identity began to be chipped away. Her true identity was being given new life!

It all started with an invitation from Jesus. Jesus said to her, "Give me a drink of water" (John 4:8 TPT).

She was expecting to be rejected by men, like she had many times before. Instead, Jesus invited Photini into a conversation by asking her to provide Him with a drink. His words surprised her so much because they defied every cultural, religious and social norm she came to expect. Jesus wanted their conversation to open up her eyes to see who she had been created to be.

Her old identity of being rejected was replaced with a new one: welcomed.

Jesus began to heal her pain from her past with His welcome. She was welcomed to engage, to share a simple drink of water with Him. She was welcomed to freely speak from her pain.

Jesus did not require perfection from her; He only desired her to feel welcomed.

I love the way the confusion over water in the natural unfolds, releasing another layer of healing of her brokenness. Photini tried to figure out how to get water from the well without cross-contamination. Even she honored the Jewish culture that held that said she, a Samaritan, was unclean, while Jesus, being Jewish, was automatically clean. She was thinking, this Jew didn't even bring a bucket, and she had no way of getting the water for him without using hers. Jesus used the normal circumstances of her life to bring her into a spiritual encounter with Him.

> "'...if anyone drinks the living water I give them, they will never thirst again and will be forever satisfied! For when you drink the water I give you it becomes a gushing fountain of the Holy Spirit, springing up and flooding you with endless life!' The woman replied, 'Let me drink that water so I'll never be thirsty again and won't have to come back here to draw water.' Jesus said, 'Go get your husband and bring him back here.' 'But I'm not married,' the woman answered. 'That's true,' Jesus said, 'for you've been married five times and now you're living with a man who is not your husband. You have told the truth'" (John 4:14-18 TPT).

Jesus was offering her a life of true oneness with Him, by being filled with the Holy Spirit and letting it bubble up in her. But first, He needed to bring healing to the shame she felt from having too many husbands, her perceived failure as a wife and not having the life of a respected woman. He did that by revealing what was hidden and acknowledging her past without condemnation.

Her old identity of shame and failure were replaced with a new one: freed!

Isn't it fascinating how Jesus took her one step at a time? As each of her un-certainties were presented, He responded with honest, straightforward words, while loving her the way His Father had created her to be loved.

The final exchange between them would set Photini on a daring journey for life. It was a journey she could have never even imagined possible for someone like her.

> "The woman said, 'This is all so confusing, but I do know that the Anointed One is coming— the true Messiah. And when he comes, he will tell us everything we need to know.' Jesus said to her, 'You don't have to wait any longer, the Anointed One is here speaking with you; I am the One you're looking for'"" (John 4: 25-26 TPT).

That was it! She got it! She dropped everything and without a minute to lose, she began to tell all the people in her town that the Messiah was here. And they all came running to encounter Him, and they BELIEVED!

The evidence of Photini's transformation from her old identity to her new identity was seeded in her heart. She now had the confidence to put the past behind her and make history by sharing the good news of Jesus with her entire town! And they all believed!

Photini was not satisfied with staying in her city, Sychar. Church history follows her journey as an apostle and an evangelist all the way to Alexandria, Egypt. As her story continues, she heads out traveling with her five sisters and two sons, beginning her missionary career.

Photini and her family were preaching the Gospel in Africa when Jesus visited her in a dream. She then set sail for Rome with her family and many other believers. Nero, the emperor of Rome, was persecuting Christians. When Nero heard of her preaching Christ, he ordered the soldier to bring her before him. Photini knew they were coming for her and went to see Nero before the soldiers could arrest her.

This is an excerpt telling the rest of her encounter with Nero:

When the emperor saw them, he asked why they had come. Photini answered, "We have come to teach you to believe in Christ." The half-mad ruler of the Roman Empire did not frighten her. She wanted to convert him! Nero asked the saints their names. Again, Photini answered. By name she introduced herself, her five sisters and younger son. The emperor then demanded to know whether they had all agreed to die for the Nazarene. Photini spoke for them. "Yes, for the love of Him we rejoice and in His name we'll gladly die." Hearing their defiant words, Nero ordered their hands beaten with iron rods for three hours. At the end of each hour another persecutor took up the beating. The saints, however, felt no pain. Nothing happened to their hands. Perplexed by the

Christian's endurance and confidence, Nero ordered the men thrown into jail.

Photini and her five sisters were brought to the golden reception hall in the imperial palace. There, the six women were seated on golden thrones. In front of them stood a large golden table covered with gold coins, jewels and dresses. Nero hoped to tempt the women by this display of wealth and luxury. Nero then ordered his daughter, Domnina, with her slave girls, to go speak with the Christian women. Women, he thought, would succeed in persuading their Christian sisters to deny their God.

Photini catechized (shared the Good News) Domnina and her hundred slave girls and baptized them all. She gave the name Anthousa to Nero's daughter. After her baptism, Anthousa immediately ordered all the gold and jewels on the golden table to be distributed to the poor of Rome.

When the emperor heard that his own daughter had been converted to Christianity, he condemned Photini and all her companions to death *by* fire. For seven days, the furnace burned, but when the door of the furnace was opened, it was seen that the fire had not harmed the saints. Next, the emperor tried to destroy the saints with poison, Photini offered to be the first to drink it. "O King," she said, "I will drink the poison first so that you might see the power of my Christ and God." All the saints then drank the poison after her. None suffered any ill effects from it.

In vain Nero subjected Photini, her sisters, sons and friends to every known torture. The saints survived ... unscathed to taunt and ridicule their persecutor. For three years, they were held in a Roman prison. Saint Photini transformed it into a house of God. Many Romans came to the prison, were converted and baptized.

Finally, the enraged tyrant had all the saints, except for Photini, beheaded. She was thrown first into a deep, dry well and then into prison again. One night, God appeared to her, and made the sign of the cross over her three times. The vision filled her with joy. Many days later, while she hymned and blessed God, Saint Photini gave her soul into God's hands."[7]

Photini said yes to Jesus's invitation to believe in Him. She RSVP'd to being transformed into a life of a godly woman, an evangelist and eventually, a martyr for the Kingdom God.

His Invitation to Us

Jesus is our invitation to everything we need pertaining to Kingdom life here on earth. He offers each one of us a second birth from our old life; we are buried, washed clean in the water and risen up in the Spirit. The second birth gives us entry into the Kingdom of God, and it imparts the ability to see through the eyes of God, so all who believe can live from His Kingdom perspective; not from the world's view.

Have you accepted His invitation of a second birth? Have you been washed clean by the water and born from above by His Spirit? If not, stop now and ask Jesus:

"Come be the Lord of my life. Teach me how to live in Your family. I am expectant! Thank You, Jesus. Amen."

---

7 http://www.orthodoxchristian.info/pages/photini.htm; (accessed 08.05.2017).

Now it is time to connect with a body of believers, like Photini, where you are able to be a part of the family in the Body of Christ and be baptized in water and in the Holy Spirit.

Water Baptism

I want to make one special note here. I have found over the years many Christians who have not been water baptized. I would encourage you to complete the process the Word sets out for us. Water baptism is a critical and power-filled part of being Born Again.

I was baptized early on with a sprinkling of water. However, after I came to understand the power of baptism by full immersion, I longed to have the Word fulfilled in my life by being immersed. I was immersed in a river that ran between two mountains during a conference in Black Mountain, North Carolina. It is here the local churches have brought their people for over one hundred years to be baptized. It was powerful! As you are immersed in the water, it becomes your invitation to bury your old self and to wash away all the things in your life that do not line up with the heart of God for you (Romans 6:3-4). When you come up out of the water, your old self stays in the water and you emerge refreshed, made new and alive in Jesus –you become a new creation! People have been healed, delivered from addictions and dramatically changed as a result of being obedient to the Word on baptism. Jesus awakens a new vision and a new understanding, and He opens a new connection to Him in baptism.

"Therefore, if anyone *is* in Christ, *he is* a new creation; old things have passed away; behold, all things have become new" (1 Corinthians 5:17 NKJV).

Benefits Only

One of the most fascinating moments with Jesus can be found in John 6, where Jesus broke every cultural norm and every status quo, including working outside of the understanding of the law. He had just finished an extended road trip where He had been teaching a crowd of thousands who had been following Him for days. He had multiplied bread on two separate occasions to feed around twenty thousand people while He healed all sickness and disease. And then He walked on water.

Many who had heard His teaching and encountered His power were only in it for the benefits of experiencing His miracles: healing and free food. So, when they asked for signs on a continual basis, He responded to their request by revealing His identity.

"Jesus said to them, 'I am the Bread of Life. Come every day to me and you will never be hungry. Believe in me and you will never be thirsty' (John 6:35 TPT).

"I alone am this Living Bread that has come to you from heaven. Eat this Bread and you will live forever. The Living Bread I give you is my body, which I will offer as a sacrifice so that all may live" (v. 51 TPT).

Being so filled with the law, there was no place for this spiritual concept to land in its followers' spirits. Not only did His words outrage those who heard, but it also triggered every fear within them. They, like Nicodemus and like many of us, were being faced with a dramatic shift in what they believed. If they followed the words of Jesus, the wall of safety they had built around their lives would have to undergo a complete renovation. And the most crucial part was that they would become like lepers and outcasts; they would no longer be accepted in their community.

Decision time was staring them down. They liked being around Him and the benefits He had to offer, such as healing, food, and wise teaching. The contradiction was glaring; they saw these signs and wonders He performed, but they could not reconcile it with the fact he was also Joseph the carpenter's son. The Jews were stuck. They could not make the transition from all they had experienced to the truth of Jesus—the Son of Man, the Bread of Life, the Living Water.

At some point in our lives, we must come to decision just like they did. What is it for you? I know that in my case, I had grown up accepting whatever I was taught about Jesus. Even though it did not resonate in me, I never questioned it. When my decision point for more of Jesus came, I was surprised I was willing, however slowly, to let go of my wall of safety. It was my moment when I made a vow to God that I would not compromise what He had called me to do for the sake for conformity. Don't misunderstand what I am saying. I never dishonored those around me; I still honored the path they chose. Even though I knew I had to turn my face toward Jesus and choose Him – all of Him.

For a time, I became the outcast in our circle of leadership. It was very difficult and at times heartbreaking. I clung to the part of John 6, where Jesus saw the mass exodus of His followers. "Then Jesus said to the twelve, "Do you also want to go away?" (John 6:67, NKJV). In that painful season of my life, the words of Peter continued to echo within me. This is my personalized version of what Peter answered, "Lord, where would I go? I have seen too much. I have encountered You, the Living God. I cannot turn away now!"

Jesus invites us into the fullness of life with all the benefits. However, there comes a time where we will be faced with a decision, like Nicodemus and Photini. Are we willing to let His truth become integrated into your spirit? This is the only way we will continue to grow in the identity and purposes He has planned for us.

I am passionate about knowing God! And not just for His benefits, but I want to know Him in a real, tangible way. I want to live out of His oneness and to help others connect in the same way. Recently, the Lord said to me that He would open the doors if I reach up and take hold of the doorknob to take what He is offering. He is good and what He gives is good too! And I want all He has. How about you?

Digging Deeper:

1. **Read John 3:1-8**

   Invite Jesus to reveal the "Nicodemus" places in you. These are places where Jesus has offered you a key to unlock His mysteries and you haven't taken it yet.

2. **Read John 4:1-30, 39-42**

   - Ask Jesus if you are holding on to an "old identity" like Photini.

   - Allow Him to show you the truth of who He created you to be.

"Love unlocks mysteries. As we love Jesus, our hearts are unlocked to see more of his beauty and glory. When we stop defining ourselves by our failures, but rather as the one whom Jesus loves, then our hearts begin to open to the breathtaking discovery of the wonder of Jesus Christ."[8]

---

8 Simmons, Brian. *John: Eternal Love (The Passion Translation)* (Kindle Locations 83-84). BroadStreet Publishing Group LLC. Kindle Edition.

Chapter 4

ONE + ONE + ONE + YOU = ONENESS

"We will come and live out life inside of you, so that you begin to see with our eyes, and hear with our ears, and touch with our hands and think like we do." —Jesus[9]

---

9 *Young, William P. The Shack (*Newbury Park, CA: Windblown Media, 2007*)*, 149.

A Glimpse of the Ones

Our first glimpse of the "we" Jesus is referring to is found in Genesis 1:1. "In the beginning God created the heavens and the earth" (NKJV). The word God translated in the Hebrew is Elohim, which is the plural form of the word. This plurality, Elohim, is not of multiple gods, but God as the Trinity: Father, Son, and Holy Spirit.

I think Robert Letham describes it well: "First and foremost, God is one being, three persons, and three persons, one being. The indivisible Trinity consists of three irreducibly distinct persons. Their distinctness or difference is in no way whatever erased, obliterated, or eroded by the union. But the union is real, eternal, and indivisible. The three are one identical being."[10]

In order to comprehend the splendor of the Trinity of God, we must embark on a journey into Their uniqueness. Right up front, the unveiling of God as Spirit is released"

"...And the Spirit of God was hovering over the face of the waters" (Genesis 1:2 NKJV).

Holy Spirit's role in context of Creation was to hover, releasing the breath of God into all living things. He is the Breath of

---

10 Letham, Robert, *The Holy Trinity: In Scripture, History, Theology and Worship*, (P&R Publishing Co., 2004), 466.

Creation! He is the Breath within the Trinity. He is the dynamic Spirit of God within all life. And He is one with us!

God also unveils Himself as the Word:

"In the beginning was the Word, and the Word was with God, and the Word was God. He was in the beginning with God. All things were made through Him, and without Him nothing was made that was made" (John 1:1-3 NKJV).

God spoke, and Creation was released through the Word: Jesus, Jesus the Son, Jesus the Creator, and Jesus the Word. God wants us to grasp the revelation that the Word is always with God, for the Word is God. Without the Word, without Jesus, nothing is made, because through Jesus, all things are created. And the Word, Jesus, is with us!

When I realized God had revealed each person of the Trinity right up front in the first lines of Genesis, I felt the holy fear of handling what was being unfolded.

In Creation, God demonstrates Their oneness, Father, Son and Holy Spirit, which continues through and in us today.

Your response may be, "Of course, that has been my understanding!"

Then, my response to you is: How has this understanding of Their Oneness in you changed your life?

For me, after months of pondering, I began to share with my closest friends what God was showing me. Once I began to talk about the beauty of Creation as a release of God – Father, Son and Holy Spirit – functioning in Their uniqueness, I saw something I had not seen before. This incredible "Ah-ha" moment sparked in me as God began to surprise me with a movie in my mind:

A room appears, but my focus is on the oversize, rectangular, wooden worktable in front of me. The table is covered with blueprints. I know they are the blueprints of Creation. It is as if each Person of God is discussing His part. There is an excitement in the air about each One bringing His part of the design to life from the Master Plan. They are ready to release the blueprint into life. The process is beginning, and I hear God the Father speak, "Heavens, rise from the blueprint of Our plans and take physical form." As the words resound from God, Jesus captures and transforms each word into Creation's equivalent. Each word is transformed, becoming animated into a breathing work of art. Silhouettes become well defined, accompanied by splashes of color with precision in identifying each one's originality. The hovering of the Holy Spirit creates a vibration rupturing the Heaven with ripples and waves of life. The magnificence of the blueprints, the Creation by the Trinity, has come to life. Their Oneness spills over every created thing. The Heavens and Earth are formed! All agree that it is good, very good! This image of a Holy Celebration flashes in my mind; all things on Earth and in the Heavens join in praising the works of the Creator.

Our Relationship with Jesus Gives Us a Clear View of Father God

Jesus was with the Father from the beginning. They have never been separate. Let us refresh our minds in this for a moment. When Jesus came to earth as a man, He was still God and was with God. The Apostle John revealed the first glimpse of this unbroken

73

union between the Father and Son. "In the beginning was the Word, and the Word was with God, and the Word was God. He was in the beginning with God" (John 1:1-2 NKJV).

This mystery of unbroken oneness between Father and Son is alluded to throughout the Word of God. However, when John experiences Their oneness, he is able to capture it with crystal-clear verbiage in the above two verses. He illuminates the exquisite eternal relationship between God and the Word.

John continues in verse 14, enlightening us with the fullness of Their relationship:

"And the Word became flesh and dwelt among us, and we beheld His glory, the glory as the only begotten of the Father, full of grace and truth" (John 1:14 NKJV).

This is just a snapshot of the Oneness between the two of them. No matter what situation Jesus was in, He was always One with the Father and He was always God. Take all this and put yourself into the snapshot. No matter what situation you are in, no matter what you face, you are one with God. Your identity has not changed, just as Jesus's identity did not change. You are a child of the Father, one with the Trinity, and part of a fearless tribe whom God needs to complete His plan.

In the previous chapter, I shared that God gave me 44 "I AM" statements about Himself. One of them was, "I Am your Father who needs you – Abba."

Have you ever thought of the Father needing us – needing me, needing you? It seems so ridiculous, the all-sufficient God in need of us. God is in need of no one. Yet God in His infinite wisdom designed us to partner with Him. Our partnership is to be like the relationship between God the Father, Jesus Christ and Holy Spirit. A oneness that brings perfect unity. Jesus came to us as a man to provide the way for us to be in this type of oneness with Them.

Our Relationship with the Father Is Birthed in Jesus

Sometimes, we read the prayers of Jesus as a son talking to His Father and we forget He is God. Through this dialog below, Jesus is telling us the way to the Father is through Him.

"To know Me is to know the Father too. If you have seen Me, you have seen the Father. And from now on, you realize that you have seen Him and experienced Him. Believe that I live *as one* with my Father and My Father lives *as one* with Me..." (John 14:6-7,11 TPT; *italics* added for emphasis).

Everything Jesus did was from His oneness with the Father. Jesus offers us the same oneness with the Father. This same oneness is made available through Him. It is the only way! This is the greatest news ever!

Take a minute and think about how you have seen Jesus interact with the Father.

Think about Their Oneness in your life.

It has been through my relationship with Jesus that I am growing in love and intimacy with God as Father. Out of this love, the movement of my life has found a synchronicity of who He is. So, what I do and say, the decisions I make are out of being in love with Him.

This, however, has not always been the case. My earthly dad was a genius and an overachiever, and he loved us kids. He was also diagnosed as bi-polar. In those days, having a mental illness brought shame. He denied the diagnosis and self-medicated with alcohol. Our home fluctuated between outrageous joy and excessive rage. My role as a kid was the TESTER. I was the one who would test dad's mood. Based on my report, we would know whether to steer clear or join him for the day. As a family, we found that the key to keep peace, to receive love and to maintain approval was perfect performance.

Because of this, it has taken time for me to be able to trust Father God's love as unconditional. I realize now, I do not have to check His mood, nor do I have to have everything perfect. I can draw near to Jesus and experience the love of Father God.

There Is Help!

There are many people who struggle to have a relationship with Father God because of the struggles they have had with their earthly father. Many times, we transfer our emotional wounding from our father to Father God. Emotional wounds are not always tied to a difficult relationship. The wounds can be linked to lies we believe about God. It is vital to discover the lies we believe and replace them with the truth. By doing so, this sets us free to receive His unconditional love. If that is the case for you, it is possible you might need assistance in this process. Help is available through inner healing ministries such as Sozo with Bethel Church, Redding, California; Christian Healing Ministries, Jacksonville, Florida; and our Healing and Encounter Rooms at The Gathering Apostolic Center, Tarpon Springs, Florida, just to name a few.

The Only Way to Know Your Identity Is to Know Jesus

I have heard it expressed this way: Jesus is a mirror, not a window. We do not look through Him; we look at Him.

Our vision must be laser-like. A single pinpoint locked on Him with exactness. It is proven that what we focus on is what we will become. When we focus on Jesus, we become like Jesus.

"... and we are being changed to be like Him... " (2 Corinthians 3:18 NCV).

"All of us! Nothing between us and God, our faces shining with the brightness of his face. And so, we are transfigured much like the Messiah, our lives gradually becoming brighter and more beautiful as God enters our lives and we become like him" (2 Corinthians 3:18 MSG).

When He is the One we fix our gaze on, it is He who reflects back in us.

Recently, I was in a meeting and the speaker gave an illustration of a racecar driver spinning out of control heading for the wall:

"In racing, they say that your car goes where your eyes go. The driver who cannot tear his eyes away from the wall as he spins out of control will meet that wall; the driver who looks down the track as he feels his tires break free will regain control of his vehicle."[11]

Are there things in your life spinning out of control?

---

11 Garth Stein, *The Art of Racing in the Rain*, http://www.goodreads.com/quotes/tag/racing, Accessed 6/15/15, 11:11 AM.

Where is your focus?

What we focus on is what we become.

If our focus is locked on feeling shame or rejection, on our overwhelming schedule, struggling with finances, or a broken relationship, we will not be able to keep from hitting the wall. If we set our focus on Jesus for whatever we need – He will provide!

Where is your focus? The way to steer clear of hitting the wall is to keep your focus on Christ! Having your eyes laser-locked on Jesus is key to an authentic transformation into His Image.

The Shack

Have you read *The Shack* by William P. Young?

When I first read it, I was stunned by his theme of Oneness. It was released in 2007 as a fiction book, and each year since, I have re-read my favorite section, starting with Chapter 5. In the story, Young identifies Father God as Papa, Holy Spirit as Sarayu and Jesus as Himself. Mack, or Mackenzie, is the main character they are drawing unto Themselves: three + one. As I read about their interactions, my spirit powerfully identified with the Oneness of the Trinity.

Here is an excerpt:

Early on, Papa explains to Mack how they, the Trinity, work together:

"We are in a circle of relationship, not a chain of command... What you're   seeing here is relationship without any overlay of power. We don't need power over the other because we are always looking out for the best."[12]

_____

12 Young, *The Shack*, 147.

How do these words line up with your understanding of the relationship of the Triune God?

As we integrate what we have just read with the Words of Christ, we see a glimpse of this circle being formed for us to join:

"But when the Helper comes, whom I shall send to you from the Father, the Spirit of truth who proceeds from the Father, He will testify of Me" (John 15:26 NKJV).

Jesus is extending His hand, joined by Holy Spirit with the hands of the Father, for us to grab hold and join with Them. And the way for us to do this is to laser-lock our eyes on Jesus. To quote the words of Jesus in *The Shack:*

"It is so simple, but never easy for you. By re-turning. By turning back to me. By giving up your ways of power and manipulation and just come back to me. I am the best way any human can relate to Papa or Sarayu. To see me is to see them. The love you sense from me is no different from how they love you."

The one thing I have found is that by turning to Jesus, trusting Him with my need, He always surprises me with the outcome. And it is always much better than I could have done myself. The solution that works for me is to keep moving forward, listening to Him and doing what He says. It sounds so simple, but believe me, it is not! IT IS NOT!

Sometimes, I just want to help Jesus by telling Him the best way to do things. Don't you?

I have a funny story to share about keeping my eyes fixed on Jesus and following God's lead. He provided me with a wonderful surprise!

79

Our leadership team was at Bethel Church in Redding, California, for "Leaders Advance" one year. As it happened, Shawn and Cherie Bolz were attending. Shawn is a well-known prophet, and at that time they were also pastoring a church in Southern California. The Lord told me to give them one of my new books, *7 Visions: A Glimpse into the Father's Heart*. Of course, my thought was, "Really God? They are here to rest and receive just like we are." In my efforts to avoid disobedience, I told the Lord, "If I run into him I will give them a book, otherwise I will mail it." Well, I did not see him that day, so I planned on mailing the book. The next morning, the Lord woke me with a prophetic word to give to Shawn and Cherie. I wrote it down, stuck it in my book and reiterated to the Lord, "If I run into them, I will give it to them; otherwise, I will mail it." I put the book in my purse and forgot all about it.

At dinner after going through the buffet line, I placed my plate on the table and glanced around; Shawn and Cheri were two tables away from me. I reluctantly picked up the book and headed over to meet them. Shawn was talking with someone else, so I decided to talk to Cherie. We had a sweet exchange, and I gave her the book and headed back to my table. Just as I sat down, I could hear my name loudly spoken by Shawn as he asked Cherie, "Where did she go?" I walked back toward him, and Shawn asked, "Is your name Cynthia? Cynthia Stewart?"

As it turned out, earlier in the day, the Lord had given him a word for Cynthia Stewart – and here I was giving *him* a word! He saved giving me my word until the meeting, but here is the funny thing. Part of the word I gave to them was confirmed to be the corporate word the Lord had given him to release that evening at the meeting. My point being, in my mind it would have been much easier to mail the book with the word, but the Lord was using both Shawn and me to confirm, encourage and release His plans. It was not only a benefit for both of us personally but for those at the Leaders Advance.

Invited into the Circle of Relationship

We are invited in to join the circle of relationship with God. This scene below is from The Shack, and it gives a pivotal understanding of God's unity from within.

Papa, Jesus, and Sarayu are all together and Mack is struggling to understand the invitation to join their Oneness in this circle relationship.

"Papa again interrupted. 'You see, Mackenzie, I don't just want a piece of you and a piece of your life. Even if you were able, which you are not, to give me the biggest piece, that is not what I want. I want all of you and all of every part of you and your day.' Jesus now spoke again. 'Mack, I don't want to be first among a list of values; I want to be at the center of everything. When I live in you, then together we can live through everything that happens to you. Rather than a pyramid, I want to be the center of a mobile, where everything in your life – your friends, family, occupation, thoughts, activities – is connect to me but moves with the wind, in and out, and back and forth, in an incredible dance of being.' 'And I,' concluded Sarayu, 'I am the wind.'"[13]

---

13 Young, *The Shack*, 207.

The Triune God invites us into a symbiotic relationship. They want us joined together in Oneness to live in true fluidity of Their love and Their best for us. Joining Their circle of relationship gives us a voice in Their interchange.

Picture it this way: You are in the circle with God – the Father, Jesus, and Holy Spirit. There will be times throughout your journey you will spend more time in communication with One than with the others. For example, you may spend time with Holy Spirit allowing your relationship to grow in love, depth and understanding. Though your time is focused on Holy Spirit, it does not change the dynamics of the circle. Father God and Jesus are still there with you as well as Holy Spirit. You are still in Oneness with all of Them. Each One is critical to bringing you into a deeper relationship with the Others. They all stay in Oneness in the circle with you regardless of Whom you are spending your time.

There is another side of this also. I struggle to find a good analogy, but here is the picture I get. Imagine the Father, Son and Holy Spirit are in this circle, and One becomes the focal point of humanity. Just as when Jesus came to earth as a man, much of the focus was on Him as it was on Holy Spirit during Pentecost. The circle of relationship remained; no One's position changed, nor did it elevate One above the Other. No! They were in agreement for Their best for mankind. We have seen this occur throughout time as God reveals His intrinsic nature and indispensable qualities of Himself: Creator, Father, Savior, Comforter, Spirit of Truth, Healer and so forth.

Have you ever worried about offending Jesus if you spent more time with Father or Holy Spirit than with Him? Ridiculous, right? Well, I have. It was because I did not understand this aspect of

Oneness between Them. As we stay in the fluidity of Their circle, we become a beautiful reflection of Them. We are to live from our relationship with every breath that we breathe, and every thought we have can grow us into a deeper oneness with Them!

An Angel's Story

I love the book by Max Lucado titled *An Angel's Story.* He brilliantly describes God's intent of bringing us into oneness through His son Immanuel. There is an ensuing battle of the angelic realm between God's army and Satan's army to get the seed of Jesus to Mary. One of the most visual phrases in the book describes the angelic battle:

"Wings flapping against wings.

Angels bumping into angels."

Can't you just feel the clashing of good against evil?

Here is a short excerpt of the Father's exchange with Satan, as He revealed the plan of birthing Immanuel whose name means God with us:

"Immanuel?" he (Satan) muttered to himself, then spoke in a tone of disbelief. "God with us?" For the first time the hooded head turned squarely toward the face of the Father. "No. Not even You would do that. Not even You would go so far."

"You've never believed Me, Satan."

"But Immanuel? The plan is bizarre! You don't know what it is like on Earth! You don't know how dark I've made it. It is putrid. It's evil. It's..."

"It is MINE," Proclaimed the King. "And I will reclaim what is mine. I will FEEL what my creatures feel. I will SEE what they see."

God spoke, " I love My children. Love does not take away the beloved's *freedom*. But love takes away fear. And Immanuel will leave behind a tribe of fearless children. They will not fear you or your hell."[14]

I love these words – "tribe of fearless children." This is what Jesus came to make us! Becoming part of His Tribe opens the door for us to have a "Three + one" life. They, Father, Son and Holy Spirit, are the Three and you are the plus one! In John 17:21-23, Jesus shares how this works. Allow me to paraphrase His words:

Abba, Our plans are unfolding just as We designed them. Father, hear My heart, as I pray not only for those who have been with Me, but I include those who will come to believe in Me. All the believers, each one, will enter into oneness with Us. And this will be the testimony to all that You have sent Me. The glory You have given to Me, I give to those who believe so they will be One with us, as You and I are One. I am in You, Father, and You are in Me. Father, I have placed My heart inside of them so we are all One. You love them in the same way You love Me, and flowing from Our love they will be able to move into perfect oneness with Us.

Each word springs to life as Jesus releases a Kingdom principle no one has ever heard. Jesus's intimate exchange with the Father unveils the Father's love for Him. Their extravagant love extends

14 Lucado, Max, *An Angel's Story* (Nashville, TN: W Publishing Group,2002), 22, 14-15.

the invitation for us to join in. Jesus's tender love for the Father spills over on us, not only for us to be loved, but to live out of His love! Does Their intimate love strike a chord with your longing for deep, authentic love? Jesus has invited us into a love relationship with the Father, with Holy Spirit and Himself. Our YES to Jesus makes the way for us to become ONE with Them.

Take a moment and allow your spirit to contemplate Three + one. Invite Jesus to give you a fresh glimpse of the intimate love They have for you. Amazing love!

Digging Deeper:

Here are some objectives for growing deeper in Oneness:

1. Describe your relationship with each person of the Trinity: Father, Son and Holy Spirit.

2. How do you see yourself in their circle of relationship?

3. Read John 17:21-26.

   - Journal regarding all the places where Jesus prays to the Father about you being joined as one with Them.

   - How does His words impact your understanding of oneness?

Chapter 5

Easy as 1, 2, 3

"Only those who will risk going too far can possibly find out how far one can go." —T. S. Eliot[15]

15 Elliott, T.S. "Brainy Quotes". https://www.brainyquote.com/quotes/quotes/t/tseliot161678.html (accessed 10.23.17)

went away for a few days to write these next couple of chapters. It is a funny thing with me; when I go away, it takes time for me to settle down from the busyness of my schedule. In my first 24 hours away, I read two books, went for a run, took a nap, went on several walks, went swimming and finally, after all that, I was ready to write. I started by reading through my previously written chapters, making additions and fine-tuning my thoughts.

Next, I opened my Bible to John 14. I began to read, stopping to ponder verses 12-14.

> "I tell you the timeless truth: The person who follows me in faith, believing in me, will do the same mighty miracles that I do – even greater miracles than these because I go to the Father! For I will do whatever you ask me to do when you *ask me* in my name. And this is how the Son will show what the Father is really like and bring glory to Him. Ask me anything in my name, and *I will do it* for you!" (TPT)

I read it over and over. Originally, I had planned something else for this chapter, but I knew the Holy Spirit wanted us to explore the question: What can we ask for? He also seemed to want us to know the why for His answers.

Sometimes, my best brainstorming happens while I sleep. Since it was 10:00 P.M., I felt like the Lord would prepare me for writing through the night, so I prayed, "Lord, give me revelation about asking and receiving." I read John 14:12-14 again, then went to sleep.

I awoke at 1:23 A.M. and I heard the Lord say, *"Easy as 1, 2, 3."*

Easy as 1, 2, 3, I repeated as I grasped for understanding. I knew He was giving me the title for this chapter, so I grabbed my laptop and began writing. Again, I told the Lord I desperately needed His insight, revelation and just as important, application to clearly release this truth of asking and receiving for our daily lives.

"So, Lord, what does it mean Easy as 1, 2 3?" The Lord showed me in the Book of John, chapters 14, 15 and 16. Jesus told His disciples **four different times** to ask and they would receive what they have asked! Jesus explained to the disciples there were reasons they should ask. And every answer they received carried a purpose much greater than what they were able to understand.

As we look at each of these four accounts individually, I am asking

Just Say "Amen"

I heard Bishop Joseph Garlington speak about understanding the ways of God, and I believe it will help you as we delve into these Scriptures. Bishop Garlington talked about how sometimes you have to come outside your constructs, your norm, to come into what God is doing. And, as we come in, we have to adjust our feelings to the facts. Furthermore, when God offers us something we do not fully understand, we are to say, "Amen" in agreement to His truth. Our comprehension is not a prerequisite to our cooperation. In other words, we don't have to know how it works; we just have to know it works! With that said, let's dig in!

the Holy Spirit to bring you understanding and practical application for you to experience these truths. There are incredible testimonies included to give you a taste of what God does when you ask!

Foundation: Believing

We need to build the foundation first.

"I tell you the timeless truth: The person who follows me in faith, believing in me, will do the same mighty miracles that I do – even greater miracles than these because I go to the Father!" (John 14:12 TPT).

First, we are to believe in Jesus! The undergirding for this comes from verse 11, "Believe Me that I am in the Father and the Father in Me..." (*Italics added for emphasis*, NKJV). Even though He is standing in the same room with His disciples, Jesus is in the Father. Jesus is in the Father and the Father is in Him. This is how you are positioned too: in Jesus, who is in the Father and the Father is in Him. Hard to grasp? Take a moment and try to visualize this.

In our intellect, capturing the understanding of being in someone is tricky. Especially when the concept of "in" denotes a fixed position. I remember one of my Sunday school kids asking how Jesus, a grown-up, was going to fit in his heart. Looking back, it was a funny question. Nevertheless, the thought of how a grown man lives in our heart is as much of a stumbling block as Jesus in the Father and the Father in Jesus. The grasping of in is critical for our forward movement to believe, as well as for our relationship with the Ones with whom we share the same spiritual space.

Think of yourself with Jesus in you and the Father in Jesus in terms of the Internet. In today's electronic age, we can all have the latest electronic equipment, but without the connection to the World Wide Web, we are isolated and restricted from our full capacity. It is this invisible yet powerful connection that allows our capabilities to explode with innumerable possibilities where we find ourselves presented with a whole new way of life. Using this technology analogy, God's Internet calls for us to be connected to Father God by believing in Jesus. Through the Holy Spirit, we are in Jesus, who is in the Father, and They are in us.

The word "believing" in the New Testament comes from the Greek *pisteuō*, which means to have confidence, have faith in, to trust, and to believe to be true. Jesus is telling us believing unlocks the door to asking and receiving. Believing is being fully convinced in your heart.

Hebrews 11:1 teaches us, "Faith means being sure of the things we hope for and knowing that something is real even if we do not see it" (NCV).

It is difficult for us to grasp the unseen; nevertheless, we can unpack the words in Hebrews as an application for Them in us and us in Them just by looking all around us. We are living on earth, which was created by the invisible spoken Word of God and yet, we see the tangibility of the ground, the oceans, and the sky. We see the product of the Word spoken. Now, apply this truth to our state of living with the Triune God in us and us in the Triune God. We received this Kingdom reality with a heart belief. And from our belief comes a synchronized relationship lived out of oneness with the Triune God. Just as the Word of God, Jesus, created the heavens and the earth, the Word of God, Jesus, has spoken to us to believe in Him and to believe in His position in the Father. This enables us to ask from a rightful position—a position of understanding that you are in Him and He is in you and you all are in the Father.

Are you trying to figure out what the works and greater works look like? All you have to do is look back on your life and throughout history to see His works are a living reality. When I am speaking, I ask my audience the following questions:

How many know someone who has been supernaturally healed?

How many here have been supernaturally healed?

How many have prayed for someone and they have been healed?

How many have shared the gospel?

How many have heard or seen someone raised from the dead?

How many have received supernatural provision?

Their responses are vibrant! Their expressions come alive with excitement to share their supernatural experience. With hands flying up, voices echoing in agreement, they answer as the entire place is filled with celebration.

We are living in the time of the works and greater works which Jesus promised. Look at the move of God across the globe. Salvation is happening by the hundreds of thousands, and in some cases, millions, every day. The stories of multiplication and people being raised from the dead are on the rise, too. Testimonies of people being translated, or in other words, supernaturally traveling from one place to another, (such as when Philip suddenly found himself with the Ethiopian) are becoming commonplace. It is what Jesus promised to all who believe in Him -- He who is in the Father and He who is in us.

Here are a few testimonies to stir up your desire for greater things:

Our church has Healing and Encounter Rooms and every time – EVERY TIME – we open our doors, we see these works and greater works of Jesus come alive. Our team gathers an hour before we open to hear from God, take Communion and share what the Lord has shown each of us. We are always amazed, because the Lord gives us words of knowledge for the type of healing (physical, emotional or spiritual) needed for that day. As the people arrive and write their requests, we are so excited to see what they have requested aligns with what God has shown us. We have come to understand that what Jesus shows us He accomplishes!

Great is our God!

Recently, we had a woman in her forties, Cathy, come who had been experiencing daily pain due to a metal rod placed in her back after an accident over fourteen years ago. Due to the rod, she was unable to bend over. After we prayed for her, she was able to bend over, her fingers almost reaching her toes – with NO PAIN!

We had another person who came in and was emotionally broken. Ingrid went into our Glory Tent crying and came out refreshed, healed, and restored by the Presence of God.

These are the greater works Jesus promised us and they are birthed from our believing Jesus is in us. We need to quit looking for and waiting on the greater things to happen. We need to recognize we are living in the times of the works and greater works! Remember, Jesus is in you, so be ready and willing to release the works and greater works to everyone you encounter!

What and Why #1

Now we get to the exciting part: the **WHAT** we can ask for and the **WHY** of His answer.

"For I will do whatever you ask me to do when you ask me in my name. And this is how the Son will show what the Father is really like and bring glory to Him. Ask me anything in my name, and I will do it for you!" (John 14:13-14 TPT)

"Just ask Me — whatever — just ask Me — and I will do it for YOU!"

What do we need to ask for? **WHATEVER!** You can ask for whatever. There is no hidden meaning in the word *whatever*. *Whatever* indicates limitless possibilities!

Why does Jesus answer your **whatever**?

Jesus answers our prayers to bring glory to the Father. See this! His answer to our whatever we ask in His Name brings glory to His Father. I am excited that Jesus extends the works and greater works offer to each of us by inviting us to ask Him anything, really anything. However, I have realized His offer comes with a caveat. The caveat being, what we are asking for will bring glory to the Father.

Jesus also answers our prayers so our joy may be full.

"Until now, you have asked nothing in My name. Ask, and you will receive, that your joy may be full" (John 16:23-24 NKJV).

The reason we can have joy in the answer is because of relationship with the Triune God. Joy is found in the deepest, innermost place of our relationship with Him. Joy is not a response interdependent on the circumstances around us. Joy is birthed out of the reality of God in us and us in Him. We are confident in the relationship knowing we are to ask Him and we are to receive from Him. Everything from the beginning of our prayer, to the in-between, to the culmination, is in His capable hands.

This is a win-win! So, when you ask Him, He will give it to you bringing glory to the Father and filling us with joy filled to the brim! Our request provides Jesus the opportunity to display the beauty, majesty and glory of the Father. Our request provides us with cascading of joy flowing that can only come from Jesus.

Ponder with me for a moment.

Let's imagine the celebration when our answer comes. Jesus brings honor, glory, and exaltation to the Father and in all the praise, comes an outpouring of joy into us. All the joy, clapping of hands, jumping up and down, shouting, dancing will be for one purpose: to direct all eyes, everyone's attention to bring glory to the Father. He is the one who made it all possible!

Following are a few more of the testimonies we have had, and I am excited to see all the works and greater works of Jesus invade so many lives. As you read them, give glory to the Father!

Someone:

- Healed of sciatic nerve pain

- Received the Baptism of the Holy Spirit
- Encountered a tangible touch of the Presence of God
- Received freedom from fear of going home
- Healed of stomach pain for 6 years
- Healed of a diabetic genetic issue

As I have realized the importance of Jesus bringing glory to Father, I catch myself asking two questions:

Will my request of Jesus bring glory to the Father?

Do I really understand the bigger picture in what I am asking?

What and Why #2

What else can we ask for?

Jesus tells us to *ask for what we desire.*

In John 15:7, Jesus tells the disciples once again to ask Him for what they need.

"But if you step into my life in union with me and if my words live powerfully within you, then you can ask whatever you desire and it will be done" (John 15:7 TPT).

Interestingly, this word desire is used in Psalm 37:4, "Delight yourself also in the Lord, And He shall give you the desires of your heart" (NKJV). In context of John 15:8 and Psalm 37:4, there is an abiding relationship that kindles a response as we set our desires before the Father in asking Him to fulfill them. Desire is beyond the needs to survive each day, such as food, clothing, and shelter. A desire is a petition attached with an ardent feeling of longing as we bare our souls completely before the Lord and wait for His yes.

God surprises us with His fulfillment of our desires, and sometimes we just need to be ready to receive in a way we do not expect. Let me share an example of God fulfilling a desire in a way I did not expect.

I love lists! I have a "Dreaming with God" list, a "Top 50 Desires" list, a Bucket list and other lists too numerous to mention. One desire on my Bucket List was to write books that would inspire and help people encounter God in the same way other books have encouraged me. It was not really something I thought I could do, since I have more of a math brain than a word brain. In school, I had a terrible time with grammar and I figured I could never write. Sometimes God surprises you by starting you out slowly and the next thing you know, your book is being published. That was exactly what happened to me! I found myself being asked to speak at different places so I needed to write out what I was going to say. Then God gave me the inspiration for an eight-week class I had to write and teach. Next, I found myself writing a weekly blog unbelievable! God also opened a door for me to attend a writer's workshop with several well-known published authors.

After two years of writing my blog, God instructed me to take certain topics, polish them and add finishing touches. I then took each title, wrote it on a sticky note and God ordered them, as they would appear in a book. I found a publisher through my friends, and so around midnight on a Saturday, I emailed my manuscript. By Monday morning, I had a message in my voicemail stating they were excited about my manuscript and wanted to publish my book! My dream was realized. What I thought impossible, God accomplished! I have so many more examples of this. He surprises me continually by fulfilling the desires of my heart. What I have found in all these years is that God hears these desires and He answers them. And many times, it is in a way you least expect it, and it is always a zillion times better than you could have imagined!

Why Does Jesus Answer Your Desires?

"When your lives bear **abundant fruit**, you demonstrate that you are my mature disciples who glorify my Father!" (John 15:8 TPT).

It is so we can demonstrate that we belong to Him by our fruit-producing lives. Not just some fruit, but **abundant fruit** – more than enough, ample, lavish, abounding, overflowing LOTS OF FRUIT!

"You did not choose Me, but I chose you and appointed you that you should go and bear fruit, and that your fruit should remain, that whatever you ask the Father in My name He may give you" (John 15:16 NKJV).

Abundant fruit happens because we were chosen and appointed to receive the answers to our request. And this abundant fruit will have a lasting impact! Whatever God does for you, it becomes your testimony of God's calling on your life and the provision of abundant fruit is the evidence for others to taste and see the goodness of the Father.

A great example of abundant, lasting fruit would be John G. Lake's healing rooms. The healing rooms were birthed from Lake's union with Jesus because Lake believed and acted on Scripture. Even though his healing rooms did not continue after his death, they produced long-lasting fruit.

You see, in 1999, Cal Pierce went to the grave of John G. Lake in Spokane and there he prayed until he received John G. Lake's anointing for healing and healing rooms. After he received the anointing, Cal traveled to different cities to release this anointing. He came to our area when he first started this venture, and I received a deposit of this healing anointing. As Cal shared the mandate God had seared in him, he announced he hadn't come to pray healing and leave, but rather he had come to make a deposit of healing in this area. My excitement was uncontainable; from that impartation, I was able to open our healing and encounter rooms. Today, the International Healing Rooms are training people all over the world with millions being healed! This is what God is offering us; He will give us abundant fruit in response to our asking for what will bring glory the Father. We are history makers for the Kingdom of God. Our personal abundant fruit releases seeds forever here on earth while being recorded in our story in Heaven. (I talk about this in my book 7 *Visions: A Glimpse into the Father's Heart*.)

God's answers to our prayers reverberate for all of eternity.

Responsibilities of Partnership

The **What and Why** seem simple – even black and white. However, there are a few remaining areas we need to explore in order to see the bigger picture. There is a partnership between Him and us. We have our responsibilities to add to the partnership.

First responsibility is to choose the words of Christ to live powerfully in you.

- His words are right and true. (Psalms 33:4)

- His words bless us to hear and obey. (Luke 11:28)

- His words direct our steps. (Psalms 119:105)

- His words give us life. (John 6:63)

Jesus is the Word and the Word in the original Greek New Testament is the *Logos*. Its basic translation is "word - implying a thought." All Scripture is recognized as Logos or the written Word of God. However, there is also yet another meaning for the word – *rhēma*. *Rhēma* is also Greek. *Rhēma* means to have been uttered by a living voice, things spoken. Jesus is giving us, along with His written *Logos*, an active word – *rhēma*. God's word is the living mechanism for the words of Christ to live powerfully in you.

My friend, Apostle Nelia Crane, called me to give me a *rhēma* word from the Lord and she said, "I don't know what this means, but here goes ... integrated sequences of words and it is important for you to capture it."

I believe her word can be applied here:

Christ becomes integrated in us; Him in us and us in Him, fused in our lives constructing a formidable relationship. And the sequence follows when you choose to live by His logos, while listening for His rhēma word.

Second Responsibility is to Be a Friend to Jesus

"You are My friends if you do whatever I command you. No longer do I call you servants, for a servant does not know what his master is doing; I have called you friends, for all things that I heard from My Father I have made known to you" (John 15:14-16 NKJV).

His friendship is one of the most intimate gifts Jesus offers to us in the deepest, truest way. This friendship Jesus offers fulfills one of His deepest desires, because our friendship with Jesus is birthed out of our obedience. When God calls us to be obedient, He is asking for us to be a good friend. Jesus is calling us to make a critical shift in our thinking. No longer are we to consider ourselves servants – performance – driven for Him. Unlike our natural performance-driven relationships, i.e., bosses, parents, co-workers, He just wants us to be His friend. We are to be relationally driven.

What does friendship with God look like? There are some definite differences from the social friendships we have today. Our friendships today are based on mutual affection for one another. Our friendship with God is not based on mutuality; it is based on sovereignty, and it is the ultimate plan He has for us. He sovereignly planned for us to be His friend. God is saying, "I have chosen friendship with you."

Friendship with God can also be defined as all in. We see this through the life of Abraham. He was all in or fully committed to God. He left his family and his country to be obedient to God's voice. Years later, while still childless, Abraham was unable to see a way for God's promise that he would become Father of the Nations to become reality, yet he still believed. It is because of this kind of obedience and belief that Abraham became known as a friend of God. He was completely devoted to God regardless of what it looked like, regardless of his frustration, regardless of his emotions. Abraham followed and obeyed God. He was the proto-type of one who fulfilled Jesus's words; "You are My friends if you do whatever I command you."

Say it out loud: **I am a friend of God!**

Third Responsibility: Steward His Revelation

Jesus has shared with us what He heard directly from the Father. He has given us understanding of the Father's heart. This revelation gives us insight in to how to ask and receive His best!

God reveals to us each day as we engage with Him. It could be as simple as reminding us to go back and grab our lunch as we are heading out the door; or to look between the cushions on the couch for our keys.

Yet God's revelation can be as complex as revealing to us how to carry a prophetic word for the future. I'll share this word God gave me in December 2015.

I saw: *Trump on a winning ticket.*

I said, "God, what do I do with this?" I prayed and watched. When it came time for the Primaries in March 2016, I went to the voting booth with the intention to vote for Ted Cruz. But then God said to me, "Do you remember what I showed you?" Of course, I did; I had thought about it over and over! So, I cast my ballot for Trump instead. He said, "Cruz will drop out of the race." I couldn't even imagine, but within weeks, Cruz had dropped out.

God said, "It is not about the man; it is about My move."

Our responsibility is to steward the revelation God gives us, whether we understand or not.

Remember, **Christ chose us!** He anointed and appointed us to take what He has heard from the Father and to run with it! Everyone not only has the opportunity to be chosen, but to hear what Jesus heard. Jesus is looking for those who will be obedient to His Word, follow His leading and lean in as He shares what the Father has spoken. This is for us for our benefit, as His friends.

Easy as 1, 2, 3 – ABSOLUTELY!

Digging Deeper:

This chapter has much to ponder and pray through. Now, it is time to activate these keys in your life.

- Write down the **What** to ask for and the **Why** for each Scripture.

  John 14:12-14

  John 15:7-8

  John 15:14:16

  John 16:23-24

- Begin to ask Jesus for your What and record the answers.

Chapter Six

Bi-Locational

"Science without religion is lame; religion without science is blind." —Albert Einstein[16]

16 https://www.brainyquote.com/quotes/quotes/a/alberteins161289.html (accessed 9.25.17)

Imagine being in two places at once
— being bi-locational!

Merriam-Webster defines bi-locational as the state of being or the ability to be in two places at the same time. Think about it this way: The Four Corners Monument is where Colorado, New Mexico, Arizona and Utah meet. You can literally stand in two states at the same time and be bi-locational. If you stretch a little, you can stand in all four states. You get the picture, right? Bi-locational!

Jesus taught His disciples about becoming bi-locational, just as He was. "Believe Me that I am in the Father and the Father in Me..." (John 14:11 NKJV). While He was here on earth, He was also in Heaven. Jesus told His disciples that He is in the Father and the Father is in Him, even though He was standing in the same room with the disciples.

Can you imagine the conversation running through their minds?

"How can this be possible for Jesus to be in the Father since the Father is in Heaven?

And how is it the Father is in Jesus? How can He be here on Earth and in Heaven, too?"

The revelation Jesus was sharing was way beyond what their natural minds could comprehend.

In his book, *Quantum Glory,* Phil Mason puts it this way: "The regenerated human spirit, supernaturally joined [or entangled] with the Spirit of God, is similarly in two places at one time." "He who is joined to the Lord is one spirit with Him" (1 Corinthians 6:17). As a result of the miraculous new birth, my human spirit, which is the real me, is now in heaven just as Jesus was in heaven even when HE was on the earth. Paul says, "Our citizenship is in heaven" (Philippians 3:20).[17]

It was their spirit that connected them to His words, for His words are Spirit and Life. As believers, we have a hard time grasping this truth of being bi-locational! Over the next few pages, we will venture together to look at this revelation of being bi-locational.

First: **How is this possible?**

Second: **How do I live out of this truth?**

How Is This Possible?

Once we are born again it does not matter where we are physically; our spiritual state remains in Christ and He in us. Jesus goes on to explain to His disciples that although He must leave, He is not leaving them alone. No! He is asking the Father to provide the Spirit of the Living God. "...I will pray to the Father, and He will give you another Helper, that He may abide with you forever" (John 14:16 NKJV). The Holy Spirit, the Living Presence of God, lives inside all who believe. This could only happen after Jesus died on the cross, lay in the grave, and rose from the dead. Once Jesus

17 Mason, Phil, *Quantum Glory: The Science of Heaven Invading Earth,* (Maricopa: XP Publishing, 2010), 319.

ascended to Heaven and joined the Father, all was accomplished for the Holy Spirit to take up residence in those who would believe in Jesus. This is what birthed the spirit to Spirit connection: our spirit to the Holy Spirit through our belief in Jesus.

Jesus continues to reveal the spirit to Spirit connection, which involves God the Father, God the Son and God the Holy Spirit. With the release of the Holy Spirit to live in us, Jesus speaks to the Father about oneness, "You, Father, are in Me, and I in You, that they also may be one in Us," and Jesus repeats the prayer, "I in them, and You in Me, that they may be perfect in one" (John 17:21, 23 NKJV).

Sit back for a minute and read this last Scripture again:

"You, Father, are in Me, and I in You, that they also may be one in Us."

Then Jesus repeats the prayer,

"I in them, and You in Me, that they may be perfect in one."

Ask the Holy Spirit to bring a deeper understanding to what Jesus is saying. Jesus is talking to you. He wants you to understand God has given you the Holy Spirit to live in you. His Presence also unites us with Father God and Jesus Himself. They are a package deal!

We can better understand these layers of revelation unveiled through what Paul refers to as "spiritual things" in 1 Corinthians 2:10-12:

"The Spirit searches all things, even the deep things of God. For who knows a person's thoughts except their own spirit within them? In the same way, no one knows the thoughts of God except the Spirit of God. What we have received is not the spirit of the world, but the Spirit who is from God, so that we may understand what God has freely given us" (NIV).

These spiritual things can only be understood through the presence of the Holy Spirit in us. No one can understand these deep things of God without the Holy Spirit.

How Do I Live out of This Truth?

There are very practical ways to live out the truth of Christ in us. We will touch on these later. However, before we do, we have to start with where and how we are positioned.

I gave the example of the Four Corners at the beginning of this chapter; now, let us apply it to the spiritual positioning of all believers. Jesus tells us where He is going – to be with the Father in Heaven, and that we will be with Him also. This is not limited to our being with Him in Heaven after we die, but because He ascended, we too ascend and become seated at the right hand of God. We ascend with Him, because our regenerated spirit is in Christ, having been born again.

"He [God] raised Him from the dead and seated Him at His right hand in the heavenly places" (Ephesians 1:20 NKJV).

These next two Scriptures establish our position in Christ as He sits in heavenly places.

"But God, who is rich in mercy, because of His great love with which He loved us...made us alive together with Christ...and raised us up together, and made us sit together in the heavenly places in Christ Jesus" (Ephesians 2:4-6 NKJV).

"If then you were raised with Christ, seek those things which are above, where Christ is, sitting at the right hand of God. Set your mind on things above, not on things on the earth. For you died, and your life is hidden with Christ in God" (Colossians 3:1-3 NKJV).

Through these Scriptures we can believe, in faith, for bi-locational living to be a reality. Though you may not completely grasp this, the Word of God and the Holy Spirit will continue to unfold this for you. Maybe this will help clarify your understanding. We are spiritual beings. We are not a body with a spirit; we are a spirit with a body.

> *"We are not human beings having a temporal spiritual experience; we are spiritual beings having a temporary human experience." —John Paul Jackson*

In order to implement the fullness of God in our daily lives, our understanding must be expanded to include the truth of who we are. Being a spirit man having a temporary human experience gives us the ability to comprehend our spirit to Spirit relationship. Our spirit is interwoven with the Spirit of the Living God and His with ours. This enables us to be positioned in Heaven, hidden in Christ at the right hand of the Father.

Set your attention on this for a moment and give yourself permission to visualize yourself seated with Jesus. There you are with the Ones who love you, surrounding you, the Godhead. They supply everything you need: peace, wisdom, and wholeness. They are with you. Because you are one with the Triune God, everything that is filtered through your spirit has the touch of God on it and is encased in Presence. You are positioned with the Godhead that supplies everything you need.

God has surprised me several times with visions of Heaven. I write about some of my experiences in my book, *7 Visions: A Glimpse into the Father's Heart* in great detail. One of the things I realized in my encounters was a shift in my perspective. My perspective went from looking up to Heaven to walking with Jesus in Heaven. In one of the visions, the Lord took me through rooms filled with supplies and super-abundance that were ready for us to access to bring to earth. There was a room filled with body parts for healing, a room with blueprints and plans, a room of treasures, and a room of miracles; do you get the picture? You can see from Jesus's perspective, because you are seated in heavenly places with Him. This revelation truly changes the way we live on earth. For me, seeing the body parts in Heaven made me realize the ability to access what I need is at my fingertips.

I saw the actualization of this in my life when I prayed healing for a friend's hips.

Several years ago, Elisabeth had fallen down the stairs and since then had continual issues with her hips. She was no longer able to jog; walking long distances was at best painful. It had taken several months of therapy just to get her able to stand relativity straight. It was obvious when her hip moved out of place. The right side would sit about an inch higher than the other side. As I prayed, God showed me a vision of the body parts room again and I saw hips with her name on them. In faith, with a prophetic action, I reached up and grabbed the pair of hips and brought them down. In another prophetic action, I laid my hands on her hips as though I were putting the new hips on her. In an instant, she remarked that her weight shifted and had become evenly distributed on both feet, and the pain in her right hip was gone! Some two years later she was still testifying that her hips had not shifted nor caused her pain since the day she received the new hips. As a matter of fact, she has begun riding her bike, which she was unable to do since her fall, almost 10 years ago.

Case Study

God has been giving me incredible revelation about the real, tangible way He supplies our needs. This is what Jesus was demonstrating for us so we could understand and apply it to our lives as well. The exciting news is Jesus's time on earth has given us clarity regarding how to operate out of our spiritual position. We, like Him, are filled with the Holy Spirit, who gives us a direct line to our Father. We too have the same access Jesus had, actually even more so, because Jesus ascended into Heaven. Plus, He said we would do even greater things because He has gone to the Father. Our access, our supply, our wisdom and the greater things are all obtained through our bi-locational position. We are in Him and He has provided complete access for us.

Let us discuss the surplus of Heaven! All four Gospels record the event of Jesus feeding five thousand men plus women and children after they left Nazareth. In Matthew and Mark, we see another event of Jesus feeding four thousand men plus women and children near the Sea of Galilee. With the amount of food available it would have been impossible to feed an estimated twenty thousand people, yet it happened, and with leftovers! On the first occasion, Jesus only had five loaves of bread and two fish, and on the second occasion, He only had seven loaves of bread and a few small fish. In both events they were faced with the ultimate equation that needed a solution.

A - fish, B -loaves, C - hungry people,
$\underline{HF}$ - the Heaven factor; the Presence of God,

GAP - God's Abundant Provision

$(A+B) / C \times \underline{HF} = GAP$

The sum of the fish and bread divided by the number of people multiplied by

the Heaven Factor or the Presence of God

Equals God's Abundant Provision for all.

The surplus of heaven comes out of our bi-locational reality. To help understand bi-locational reality, look at Acts 17:28, "For in him we live and move and have our being" (NIV). And we know, "For in him, all things were created: things in heaven and on earth, visible and invisible" (Colossians 1:16 NIV). The invisible, like the multiplication of the bread, though unseen in the natural, materializes once it is acknowledged through our bi-locational lifestyle.

Our bi-locational lifestyle is not only for calling forth the unseen, but also for putting that which is seen in the light of eternity. Remember, spiritually we live a bi-locational reality all the time, 24/7. Our awareness of this bi-locational reality thrives as we grow in fellowship with Christ in us. This partnership with Christ flows into our reality of our everyday life, affording us opportunities to practice and activate what He has demonstrated for us. The outcome of bi-locational living gives us supernatural access to bring Heaven to Earth, transforming the world around us!

Quantum Physics Agrees

Quantum physics identifies laws and principles, which confirm our bi-locational existence and the miracle of calling the unseen into reality. This is the HF – Heaven Factor, in our equation; our co-laboring with the Presence of God. David Van Koevering explains that because of the laws of quantum physics, our spoken intent can bring something from the unseen realm into the seen and we can make the non-material appear in material form. In other words, we can "pop qwiffs." There is a non-physical reality from which this universe and everything in it flows.

> "Popping a qwiff is a quantum physics term for the transformation of a wave into a particle by the intent of the observer. In other words, everything exists as energy in a formless, wave-like state with the possibility of becoming a particle of solid matter."[18]

Keeping this in mind helps us to understand faith. "Faith is an unseen energy force. It is not matter, but creates matter and actually become matter. You have a choice to use the energy of your words to change matter." [19]

---

18 Franklin, Judy and Davis, Ellyn, *The Physics of Heaven*, (Shippensburg: Destiny Image Publishers, 2012), 145
19 Franklin, Judy and Davis, Ellyn, *The Physics of Heaven*, (Shippensburg: Destiny Image Publishers, 2012), 143, 145

In other words, everything exists as energy and energy exists in a formless wave-like state with the possibility of becoming a particle of solid matter. You can see or observe a God qwiff (something God shows you that is not yet real in this dimension) and, by observing or popping that qwiff, cause that potential to become your reality. God used faith substance and word energy to create the universe. He spoke and the vibrations (sound) of his words released (caused) the substance that became the stars and planets.

Job 22:28 is an example of the energy of the spoken word. In declaring a matter (the spoken word), it will be established for us.

In the example of multiplication, Jesus gave us new revelation by bringing the unseen into the seen. He knew the people were hungry and took what was available in the natural, the fish and the loaves, calling forth the non-material/invisible to "pop qwiffs" for 20,000 plus! Jesus lifted up the small amount of what they had to heaven. He changed its location and placed it in a dimension not of quantity, but of infinite supply. The invisible, the things God has shown us, are just a nanosecond in front of us, ready to become visible. Jesus modeled this life of intimacy with the Father to bring us into the same place He lived from and enjoyed.

Testimony of Multiplication

I recently had lunch with my friend, Dr. Kynan Bridges. We were talking about testimonies of multiplication of food when he became excited and shared what happened at his church. I asked him to send his testimony so I could include it in my book. The following is his testimony:

116

I want to share a testimony of God's supernatural abundance being manifested in our lives. One year for our New Year's Eve service, we were believing God to bring as many people as possible. Prior to this time, only around 40 people were attending our Sunday service. We began to pray for His increase. In preparation for the New Year, we printed about 150 flyers and distributed them at a local mall in our area. In addition to that, we bought some finger foods, including some chicken and sandwiches.

The day before our event, I kept sensing we were going to experience God's supernatural power. The evening of the New Year's Eve service, there were more people present than we ever anticipated. None of the people who attended had received the flyers that we had distributed; they were simply drawn by the Spirit of God. As we were about to close the service, my wife realized we had a serious problem: there was not enough food *to feed everyone. As a matter of fact, it was only enough food* to feed our staff and a few more people. My wife prayed over the food. To our amazement, people kept coming back for more and more food. Everyone ate second and third portions. We actually had enough food left over to last us a whole week. – *Dr. Kynan Bridges*

We both agreed the multiplication of the food to superabundance should not be an anomaly, it should be normal in daily life. We are to live from our position, which is bi-locational, making our location on earth as it is in Heaven!

Bringing Heaven's Dimension to Earth

Jesus provided what was needed on earth; from *revelation*, to *healing*, to *life*, and more. He was able to do this because He was filled with the Holy Spirit and lived bi-locationally. Jesus's ability to be One with the Father or in-sync with the Father stems from His position and from His relationship with the Father.

Jesus revealed the Kingdom of God in all that He did as He continually revealed Himself as the Messiah to all who encountered Him.

> "The woman said, 'This is all so confusing, but I do know that the Anointed One is coming, the true Messiah. And when he comes, he will tell us everything we need to know.' Jesus said to her, 'You don't have to wait any longer; the Anointed One is here speaking with you. I am the One you're looking for'" (John 4:25-26 TPT).

In this encounter, Jesus reveals His identity as the Messiah to Photini, the woman at the well, who then shares the revelation with everyone in town.

In the next Scripture, Peter receives the revelation from the Father that Jesus is the Messiah.

> "Then Jesus asked them, 'And who do you say I am?' Simon Peter answered, 'You are the Christ, the Son of the living God.' Jesus answered, 'You are blessed, Simon son of Jonah, because no person taught you that. My Father in heaven showed you who I am...'" (Matthew 16:15-17 NCV).

In these next two verses Jesus reveals to the disciples His position in the Father and that He and Father are One.

"Jesus explained, 'I am the Way, I am the Truth, and I am the Life. No one comes next to the Father except through union with me. To know me is to know my Father too. And from now on you will realize that you have seen him and experienced him'" (John 14:6-7 TPT).

Jesus also brought the Kingdom of God through healing.

"Then great multitudes came to Him, having with them the lame, blind, mute, maimed, and many others, and they laid them down at Jesus' feet, and He healed them" (Matthew 15:30 NKJV).

They were all healed through the Presence of Jesus. Did Jesus lay hands on each person? We do not know. What we do know is that Jesus released Heaven, where there is no sickness, no disease, and no infirmity. He took what He had accessed in the nanosecond before Him, the invisible, and brought the unseen to the seen. He changed the way they thought by teaching them to be Kingdom-minded. He brought them truth, feeding their minds and their spirits. They encountered the reality of Heaven all because Jesus understood His position and His relationship.

Take a moment and think about what Jesus does: He meets you where you are, gives you what is needed, frees you from evil intent, all so you can bring the Kingdom of God to Earth.

Jesus also provides life – because He is our life! Jesus is our life in the Kingdom. In Him is life; we live and breathe and have our being in Him. In Him, life is more than food and clothing, for those are external, temporal. His life is eternal, yet exists in us with every breath we take. In our earthly life He forgives our sins giving us new life. He literally raises the dead to life today just as He did with Jairus's daughter and with Lazarus two thousand years ago (Mark 5; John 11). For recent testimonies of being raised from the dead, read Sid Roth's *Heaven Is Beyond Your Wildest Expectations.*

Digging Deeper:

1. Find a quiet place and read through the Scripture below several times.

   "But God, who is rich in mercy, because of His great love with which He loved us...made us alive together with Christ... and raised us up together, and made us sit together in the heavenly places in Christ Jesus" (Ephesians 2:4-6 NKJV).

   - Pause between each reading until you have a picture or a sense of sitting in heavenly places in Christ.

   - Once you sense you are seated with Him, ask the Lord to help you encounter His truth and transform your thinking.

   - Write down the things He is showing you.

2. Ask the Lord to bring someone to mind who needs to be healed.

   - Imagine yourself seated with Jesus and seeing them healed.

   - Thank Poppa God for healing them.

   - Release wholeness over their body.

3. Ask the Lord to bring to mind someone who has a need for their supply to multiplied.

   • Imagine yourself seated with Jesus with the abundant supply to fill their need.

   • Thank Poppa God for His provision.

   • Release what you see into their hands.

4. Ask the Lord to bring to mind someone who has a question about the Kingdom.

   • Imagine yourself seated with Jesus receiving the answer.

   • Thank Poppa God for revelation of Heaven.

   • Share the revelation with the person.

Chapter Seven

PERFECT LIVING ZONE

"God gave us the gift of life; it is up to us to give ourselves the gift of living well." —Voltaire[20]

---

20 https://www.goodreads.com/quotes/tag/living-well (accessed 9.28.2017).

will never forget the first time I heard the phrase "Perfect Health Zone" (PHZ) from Bill Johnson, the senior leader of Bethel Church in Redding, California. My first question was, "God, is this possible?" I knew God healed. After some pondering and praying, I knew in my heart it was possible. I knew I had to go after it.

Personally, I had experienced supernatural healing for my back. I had seen others healed miraculously with my own eyes, and God had used me to release immediate healing to others.

What I didn't know was how to foster a Perfect Health Zone in my region and beyond. I had to find out how to do it!

Now, remember that in the previous chapter we learned we are seated in Heavenly places. Allow His Presence to stretch and expand while fine-tuning your understanding of life lived bi-locationally. Over the last few years the Lord began to share with me that it is not limited to a PHZ; health is only one aspect. He gave me the phrase "Perfect Living Zone" (PLZ). It includes our partnership and our cooperation with God combined with other factors to live in this PLZ.

God showed me the Perfect Living Zone is an alignment of our spirit, soul and body in wholeness with God as we live in this world. This is a little hard to grasp because of our experiences with physical, emotional and provisional struggles, but God is greater than our experience and we must not reduce who He is to validate our experience. He is releasing this revelation for our longevity so that we are available and able to bring to fruition the prophecy Bob Jones released about the Billion Soul Harvest.[21] We are to be facilitators of this harvest, but we cannot if we are weak, sick or aged. In this chapter, we will investigate life in the PLZ from different perspectives.

The Moses Principle

The Perfect Living Zone foundation is within us, our spirit. We are going to start our investigation with Deuteronomy 29:29. "The secret things belong to the LORD our God, but the things revealed belong to us and to our sons forever, that we may observe all the words of this law" (NASB). When God reveals something to us, it is ours to own and live out.

Keep this in mind as we look at the final days of Moses's life. "Moses was one hundred twenty years old when he died. His eyes were not weak, and he was still strong" (Deuteronomy 34:7 NCV). I must say, I have prayed this over my husband and myself for years, and although we are not in perfect health, we are healthy. It seems to be working!

In studying Moses's life, I realized there is a natural and supernatural side to a Perfect Living Zone. As I read on in Deuteronomy, I realized that since Moses's eyes were not weak and his body was still strong, it took the voice of the Lord commanding Moses's body to die before he did. Moses did not die of disease, sickness or old age; Moses died at the spoken Word of

---

21 http://www.breakingchristiannews.com/articles/display_art.html?ID=17591, (accessed May 14, 2018).

the Lord. Did you understand when you read about Moses dying that he was healthy and the only way for him to die was through God's command?

My next question is this (and I am sure it is yours as well): Is Moses's long life and good health, which I will call The Moses Principle, an exception or should it be the norm for us?

It is much easier to think of The Moses Principle as an exception. This way, we can move on without considering the impact this could bring to our bodies. It releases us from the responsibility of helping ourselves and helping others move into this Perfect Living Zone.

After much thought, prayer, and reading, both the Bible and other materials, I came to realize this should be our norm! So, here is my challenge to you: I am asking you to journey with me in The Moses Principle with the mindset of it being the norm for you. Will you accept the challenge?

Let me share with you the two main reasons I believe this should and could be the norm and not an exception.

First, did you know that in the United States, the life expectancy is 79 years according to the World Bank?[22] Of this, 73.8 percent of the deaths are caused by these ten factors: heart disease, cancer, chronic lower respiratory diseases, stroke, unintentional injuries, Alzheimer's, diabetes, influenza/pneumonia, kidney disease and suicide.[23]

Is it really God's best for you to die in any of these ways?

22 https://data.worldbank.org/indicator/SP.DYN.LE00.IN (accessed 10.23.17)

23 https://www.usatoday.com/story/news/nation/2014/10/08/us-life-expectancy-hits-record-high/16874039/ (accessed 10.23.17)

Push past these statistics and stop settling for this as the norm and go with the Word of God. God wants us whole for our entire life! He continually draws us near to Him and we are to live in that intimacy, which provides wholeness for us. He tells us that He is our Healer. If we are faced with any type of illness, disease, or infirmity, we are to come to Him because He heals! If you study any of the people listed below, including Moses, you will discover the one commonality they shared was their intimate relationship with the Lord. They pushed past the problems they faced, they believed what God said, then followed His instructions.

Job lived to be two hundred forty years old. Sarah lived to be one hundred twenty-seven years old. Abraham lived to be one hundred seventy-five years old. Isaac lived to be one hundred eighty years old, and Joshua one hundred ten years old. The Apostle John reportedly died at around ninety-four years of age, but he did not die of natural causes.

Secondly, in speaking with the Lord, I believe He showed me there is a life of wholeness, not just in physical health, but wholeness of our soul and wholeness in our lives which includes prospering, thriving, and flourishing.

There is a great movement of God occurring right now. It is the great harvest of people exponentially increasing: The Billion Souls Harvest! Recently, I was reading a post by Johnny Enlow from 2015. He states:

"An estimated one hundred million people became followers of Jesus Christ, including perhaps up to a half-million Muslims... The number of Holy Spirit-filled believers (seven hundred million) reached almost one in ten on the planet, which is the highest ever. The extreme poverty rate in the world dropped to its lowest ever; abortions dropped to almost one half the rate they were in 1990. Divorce rates continued their recent substantial drop. Teen pregnancies decreased to their lowest rate since 1940, when statistics were first recorded."

These numbers confirm God needs us whole!

These numbers are exciting, because they show us that the more people who follow Jesus the sooner these statistics will drop!

God needs seasoned, mature saints to be healthy and ready to disciple and mentor new believers in this time of great harvest. He is building His Kingdom here on earth, and He is looking for people who are interested in staying around long-term to participate! Our long life provides both a greater number of people to become leaders, and to help raise up leaders like Moses did with Joshua.

Glory

Review Moses's life for a moment. The linchpin to Moses's vitality and his longevity was the Glory of God. As we look at Moses's life we discover a line of demarcation, which initiated the pattern for living in the Glory. Moses was tending his father-in-law's sheep on Mount Horeb, which is another name for Mount Sinai. Horeb means desert.

Here in this desert place, Moses had a life-changing encounter with the Presence of God, which set the course for the rest of his life.

"And the Angel of the Lord appeared to him in a flame of fire from the midst of a bush. So he looked, and behold, the bush was burning with fire, but the bush was not consumed. Then Moses said, 'I will now turn aside and see this great sight, why the bush does not burn.' So, when the Lord saw that he turned aside to look, God called to him from the midst of the bush and said, 'Moses, Moses!' And he said, 'Here I am.' Then, He said, 'Do not draw near this place. Take your sandals off your feet, for the place where you stand is holy ground.' Moreover, He said, 'I am the God of your father—the God of Abraham, the God of Isaac, and the God of Jacob.' Moses hid his face because he was afraid to look upon God" (Exodus 3:2-6 NKJV).

He had realized what he witnessed was beyond the possibilities found in the natural when the fire did not consume the bush. Moses experienced a physical encounter with God as a Holy Fire. This is how the emergence of Moses's life, steeped in the glory, began. I can almost see Moses as he took one foot out of his sandal and stepped into the circle of Holiness God had prepared. But wait, he wasn't done; he slid the other foot loose of his sandal and then also placed it on this holy ground. Moses stepped into his new position of being consumed by the Holiness of God – the Glory of God.

In this encounter with God, the Lord taught Moses four critical life lessons: how to recognize God's Presence, how to enter into His Presence, who God is and how to receive his identity as a child of God. Moses had been working in this same location for forty years, and suddenly, there was a burning bush that was not consumed – that was an anomaly! Because he stopped, took the time and examined what was occurring, he encountered the Presence of God. God teaches us to recognize His Presence in a way we can perceive Him. Like Moses, we can be in our own environment when God uses something unique to stir our spirit, giving us the opportunity to look.

Moses said YES to being open to God. This is critical to entering into His Presence. Through his openness he recognized the Presence of God. Then, once he recognized it was the Lord, Moses had a choice to either see what the Lord wanted or to turn away. Moses chose to turn to see this great sight. In his turning he was essentially saying YES to God's beckoning. Moses stepped with openness in His response to God. We can be within reach of God and still miss His Presence if we do not choose to be open to Him. He never limits His wooing to capture our hearts – with God it is not a one-shot deal. He never gives us just one opportunity – He never gives up!

As Moses stood in God's realm of Holiness, it was then God spoke His identity.

"I am the God of your father - the God of Abraham, the God of Isaac, and the God of Jacob..." (ibid). As God pronounces His identity, Moses is overcome and hides his face in awe of God. Imagine Moses's astonishment as he hears the sound of God's voice declaring who He is for the very first time. Every part of his spirit, his body, his bones, his heart – every cell recognizes the One who had created them: God.

As God spoke His identity over Moses, it stirred and awakened Moses's true identity as a Levite. Though Moses was raised in Pharaoh's house, his Hebrew family nurtured him in the ways of God in his formative years. As the words of God seized Moses's heart, they rekindled the truths he had been taught as a child. Moses grew in his relationship with God and was transformed into the man God created him to be. Moses was forever changed. If you dig deeper into their relationship, you will find ongoing encounters between Moses and God.

> "Now it was so, when Moses came down from Mount Sinai (and the two tablets of the Testimony were in Moses's hand when he came down from the mountain), that Moses did not know that the skin of his face shone while he talked with Him. When Aaron and all the children of Israel saw Moses, behold, the skin of his face shone, and they were afraid to come near him. And when Moses had finished speaking with them, he put a veil on his face. Whenever Moses went in before the Lord to speak with Him, he would take the veil off until he came out; and he would come out and speak to the children of Israel whatever he had been commanded. And whenever the children of Israel saw the face of Moses, that the skin of Moses's face shone, then Moses would put the veil on his face again, until he went in to speak with Him" (Exodus 34:29-31, 33-35 NKJV).

Moses was overflowing with the Presence of God, so much so, God's glory was illuminating his skin, and he didn't even realize it until the people became afraid. It was at this point that Moses began to veil his face when he spoke to the people. Only when it was time for him to meet with God would he remove the veil. I can see a movie of this in my mind: Moses running to meet with God, ripping off the veil on his way in anticipation of speaking with God and hearing God speak. This is the intimacy, the glory zone Moses walked in through much of his life. I believe it was his time spent in the glory of God that ushered him into the Perfect Living

Zone. God's glory kept his spirit, soul and body in wholeness: in the Perfect Living Zone.

There are times I have been caught in the glory of God. I share the following to encourage your journey. In an old journal, I found an illustration of a vision I drew when I was caught in the glory of God. Immediately, when I looked at it, I was taken back into the vision. It was March 30, 2005. I was sitting in my living room and the Lord instructed me to prepare Communion and to bring my new gold band my husband had just given me. The band was engraved in Hebrew with the words from Song of Solomon 6:3, "I am my beloved, And my beloved is mine" (NKJV).

Suddenly, the Presence of the Lord captured me and took me into a vision. I was standing before Father God and was dressed in a wedding gown. It was a beautiful, white gown with a long sheer train, like a cape. Even though I was dressed for a wedding, there was no wedding party, nor guests; just a swirl of white hues all around me. The Father led me down a long aisle through a small arched, entryway into a cave. Jesus was sitting on the floor. In front of Him was a fire burning, illuminating the entire room. I intuitively took my place across from Him. To His right was a table set with a goblet of wine, a plate of bread and figs. We sat on the floor, He served me and we ate together. Jesus spoke to me saying, "Stay in My Chamber and grow in the joy of My Father under My Father's embrace."

Once we finished the meal, the scene changed and there before me was a beautifully jeweled gold crown, scepter and a throne. The jeweled scepter held what appeared to be a large diamond in the top. The royal throne displayed ornate woodcarvings on the top rail with red embroidered cushions.

The Lord spoke: "I have given you something to rule over – the hearts of My People – to bring wholeness and health to them. Cindy – Ruler of Hearts." There were several other words, but these were more impressed upon me. Each word was like a gift that floated in the air toward me. I felt supernatural love pouring into me as I opened each one. All of a sudden, angels appeared in a line, and I knew they had been given to assist me.

I share this vision as an example of what each one of us has been given – an assignment like Moses. Each of us has areas of influence called spheres we are responsible to rule over for the Kingdom of God. Our authority is to be exercised in these spheres. We are given this responsibility and authority because you are the Bride of Christ operating out of His glory!

Obedience

Glory is only one part of the Perfect Living Zone. Jesus taught that obedience shows our love for Him, and hence becomes another part of the PLZ. "Loving me empowers you to obey my word...." (John 14:23 TPT). The word obey has a broader meaning than we understand. It is the Greek word *tereo*, which means to attend to carefully, take care of, to guard, to observe, to reserve. In the Old Testament, the Lord spoke to Joshua, "Only be strong and very courageous that you may observe to do according to all the law which Moses My servant commanded you; do not turn from it to the right hand or to the left, that you may prosper wherever you go" (Joshua 1:7 NKJV). In Hebrew the word observe is translated to *shamar*, which is the same as *tereo*, to keep, guard, observe, give heed.

I want us to recalibrate our thinking when it comes to obedience. I remember when I was growing up with my four siblings.

When my dad told us to do something, we did it! And it was not because we loved him; it was because we feared him. So obedience was a form of survival! This whole concept of being empowered by love was foreign to me. Honestly, like many of us, our understanding of obedience to God stems from what we learned as children. I learned to equate fear with obedience!

Instead, God wants us to understand His perspective, which becomes clear when we understand the true meanings of the words obey or observe. He is asking us to keep, to guard, to take care of, to attend to carefully what He has asked. This response not only stems out of love, but also above all is an invitation to join Him in His glory, in the relationship and partnership He has prepared for us; this is why He created us in His image.

In His image, we are capable of bringing Heaven to Earth!

This is our inheritance!

This is our Perfect Living Zone!

This is what we were created for!

Does this change your perspective on obedience?

The next time you feel the nudge from God to follow Him, remember He is asking for obedience. He is asking you to receive your inheritance, to step into the PLZ, and to walk in what you were created to do!

Declaring His Word

Making a declaration is equivalent to lighting a stick of dynamite; it is explosive with power! When we make a declaration aligned with the Word of God and His plan, Heaven is activated to respond. "You will also declare a thing, and it will be established for you; so light will shine on your ways" (Job 22:28 NKJV). Before you get too carried away decreeing and declaring, there are a couple of foundational things you must understand for your decrees to be effective.

Decreeing in God's design is also a part of the PLZ and is connected to authority. One of the clearest examples is found in the book of Esther. King Xerxes held all authority; what he said was done without question. He delegated his authority to his right-hand man, Haman. When he learned Haman was trying to kill all the Jews, which included his wife Esther whom he loved, King Xerxes stopped his plot against Esther and the Jews by sending Haman to the gallows. The king then transferred the authority he had given to Haman to Mordecai. Here is the essence to decreeing; you decree in what is in alignment with what God says. In those days, the order would be written, taken to every town and decreed. Due to the king's authority, it would be followed without question and could not be revoked.

Esther 8:8 states,

"You yourselves write a decree concerning the Jews, as you please, in the king's name, and seal it with the king's signet ring; for whatever is written in the king's name and sealed with the king's signet ring no one can revoke" (NKJV).

We belong to the Kingdom of God, and His Kingdom authority has been delegated to us! We carry the King's signet ring by the way of His Spirit living inside of us!

Are you getting excited about this yet?

Our decrees carry the full weight of Heaven to enact and fulfill what has been declared!

There is one more element in declaring or decreeing, and it is found in the early verses of Job.

"Obey God and be at peace with him; this is the way to happiness. Accept teaching from his mouth, and keep his words in your heart. If you return to the Almighty, you will be blessed again. So remove evil from your house. You will find pleasure in the Almighty, and you will look up to him. You will pray to him, and he will hear you, and you will keep your promises to him" (Job 22:21-23, 26-27 NCV).

God wants us to get the revelation of living in these internal zones: glory, obedience and decree. Living in glory and in obedience and decreeing God's Word will bring external results. His Glory is the fire lighting our path to obedience. Combining God's glory and our obedience with declaring His Word transfers us into the Perfect Living Zone.

Digging Deeper

- You saw how Moses was filled with Glory as he met with God.

  In John 17, Jesus is speaking with the Father and we see the foundation of Glory already seeded in you. He has prepared His Glory to grow and flourish in you as you spend time with the Lord.

- Meditate on John 17:22, "For the very glory you have given to me I have given to them, So that they will be joined together as one And experience the same unity that we enjoy" (TPT).

- Sit quietly and praise God for all He has done. Give yourself permission to be drawn into the Glory of the Lord.

- Keep a journal. Remember, obedience is carefully tending to what the Lord has spoken. Record every detail God is saying to you through the Word.

  Is there anything you are sensing? What thoughts come to your mind? Write them down.

- Meditate on Psalm119: 57, "You are my Satisfaction, Lord, and all that I need; so I'm determined to do everything you say" (TPT).

- Ask the Lord if there is something He needs for you to tend carefully.

- List one circumstance that needs to be changed in your life.

  Locate a Scripture that speaks life into your need.

  For example, for your health, you could declare Deuteronomy 34:7, "Moses was one hundred twenty years old when he died. His eyes were not weak, and he was still strong." Lord, I declare that my eyes are not weak and my body is strong.

  Then list the health issue, for example, back pain, and add to your declaration.

  I declare my back is strong, all pain has to leave now and I am fully mobile.

- Commit fully to these principles and don't give up!

Chapter 8

MOVING INTO THE PERFECT HEALTH ZONE

"I believe that the greatest gift you can give your family and the world is a healthy you." —Joyce Meyer[24]

24 https://www.brainyquote.com/quotes/quotes/j/joycemeyer567639.html (10.2.2017)

God has been teaching me about the different options in keeping my physical, emotional and spiritual state whole. In the previous chapters we covered quite a bit regarding spiritual wholeness, though emotional and physical wholeness are equally important. Prayer has been my constant go-to for healing along with traditional medicines, but in the last ten years, I have also implemented alternatives such as supplements, essential oils, frequencies, and massages. I might add with great results.

My Journey of Wholeness

Several years ago, the vision in my right eye became very blurry. It was as if a film was over it, and I could barely see. I went to numerous eye doctors without success. Finally, one referred me to my medical doctor who in turn ordered a full range of tests, including testing for multiple sclerosis. After months of doctors' tests and friends praying for me, one Saturday morning, I had reached the end of my patience. I called a dear friend of mine who had repeatedly offered to help. He made a call to one of his friends who happened to be a retina specialist. On Monday morning, I was sitting in his office looking at my file labeled with big bold letters FOD. It startled me because my file was the only file that was labeled as such. Once, he finished the battery of tests, he brought me into his office and after a quick exchange about our mutual friend, he asked, "Are you a pilot or a lawyer?" To which I replied, "Neither." He continued to explain the issue with my eye was usually found in men with high-stress positions. What? When He asked me what I did for a living, I was a little embarrassed as I answered, "I am a mom and an elder at my church." Of course, I wasn't embarrassed in what I did. I was embarrassed, because I thought my life was stress-free.

What I was diagnosed with was caused by stress. I learned that I internalized stress and the effects appeared as a physical ailment in my body –the loss of vision. Stress, in general, whether it is created by excitement over fun things or challenges in life, can create physical and emotional issues. In my new season, there were many new opportunities, some requiring more education and all requiring a tighter schedule. I was enjoying it all, but they were stressors. Although good stressors, they still caused stress and I internalized it, with my eye suffering the consequences. Once I became aware of what I was doing, I began to make some adjustments regarding these stressors, and my eye was healed within months. By the way, I also found out the FOD was not a code for sickness; it was a code of endearment: Friend of doctor!

I am going to make a bold statement here, and it comes out of my burning desire for everyone to be whole. When I pray for people who need healing, I pray with an expectation they will be healed right then on the spot! I expected the same type of healing for my eye, and I know God could have healed me supernaturally, even though He did not. God is a good, good Father and out of His goodness, He gave me understanding of the source that created the physical problem. I am now aware of this stress factor that occurs in me and have been successful in managing my stress in a healthier way. I know God has given me a revelation about this, and it is my responsibility to be a good steward of what He has given me so I can live a long, healthy life. I feel I have a responsibility to share what I have learned so others have can have a healthier life, too.

Over the course of the next few years I switched to a doctor who practices functional medicine, which means they look for the underlying causes instead of only treating the symptoms. Their treatment often includes a more natural path of healing. Between prayer and my new doctor, I have been able to take care of several issues that were diagnosed as chronic and now are only occasional irritations.

One of my most remarkable healings dealt with my propensity to sinus infections. They would occur four to six times a year and always required antibiotics. That is a lot of drugs! So frustrating! I went to an ear, nose and throat specialist in the height of my struggles, and he scheduled surgery immediately. I agreed, hoping this would be my answer to what he diagnosed as a deviated septum.

Praying and thinking about this on the drive home, I realized this was not right. I knew I should not have agreed to the surgery. I had been so desperate for relief I came into agreement for surgery and was now realizing this was not my cure. I canceled the surgery upon arriving home and found a new doctor. My new doctor scheduled me for allergy testing and found my allergies were mainly due to environmental pollutants. He advised allergy pills and sprays, but I continued to battle sinus infections. I began focusing on alternative treatments such as boosting my immune system with local honey and natural vitamins. I continued to receive healing prayer. After changing doctors one more time, I was retested and this time there were no allergies detected. I am allergy-free! My sinus infections have become only an occasional occurrence. I know God is teaching me how to be a better steward of my body that I might live in His Perfect Health Zone.

There is more. Ever since I was a teenager, my back would catch whenever I bent over and then I would not be able to stand up straight for days. The doctor said it was early signs of arthritis. While at a conference in Knoxville in 2006, the speaker had a word of knowledge about God healing backs. As soon as the words left his mouth, a shooting pain went through my back. As I grabbed my back, he prayed and the pain immediately left! I have not had a catch in my back since. I have continued to seek other ways to take care of my body naturally. For example, I love to play tennis and run, and all that pounding the pavement can cause havoc on the muscles. So, I found a great massage therapist and with her help and a little ice, I can take care of all the pain and inflammation without using any chemical drugs, not even aspirin.

Life is a journey. I continue to learn better ways to steward my body with the one constant being I seek God first in attending any physical and emotional issue. Now God is sending me to help others to move into His Perfect Health Zone (PHZ). I share my testimonies to encourage you that God works supernaturally, God works naturally and God works through doctors; all these elements are a part of God's plan. All healing comes from God!

Is It Well with Your Soul?

Included in this Perfect Health Zone is wholeness for our soul. Our soul includes the heart, mind, and emotions. 3 John 1:2

says, "Beloved, I pray that you may prosper in all things and be in health, just as your soul prospers" (NKJV). In order for us have a prosperous soul we need to have what I call a soul tune-up. These regular tune-ups reveal anything the enemy has set against you through lies, false beliefs, and trauma, plus things you do not even realize that have come against you.

> "A thief has only one thing in mind: he wants to steal, kill, and destroy. But my desire is to give you everything in abundance, more than you expect--life in its fullness until you overflow!" (John 10:10 TPT)

It is clear this verse includes a very real battle for our very soul. In this verse Jesus is actually giving us a heads-up of the enemy's plan to destroy our abundant life. The enemy has a great path of access to our soul through our wounds. Many times we do not realize the enemy has penetrated our borders with his lies. These lies keep us from God's abundance. The tune-up for our soul unearths the lies, realigns us with the truth of God, and revives our soul.

After my mom passed away, I became passionate to understand more about supernaturally healing. I read everything I could get my hands on until I realized I needed hands-on training. When I enrolled in a Christian healing school, my initial goal was to learn how to pray for physical healing. Fortunately, the school included healing of the soul or emotional healing, too. This is healing for our hurts, hang-ups, wounds and lies. Once these are uncovered and dealt with by the Holy Spirit, we find freedom. I learned and experienced this healing power of the Holy Spirit personally. During the practicum, I saw the Holy Spirit shine light on the hidden things that were holding people back. Through a process of recognition, forgiveness, and receiving the truth, each person was set free. I was stunned! I realized this was integral to living in wholeness.

Immediately, I put what I had learned into action. I marveled at the healing I witnessed. Each healing stirred a greater hunger in me to learn more. I sought training at places that had break-throughs in the areas I sought. I had come to realize the more healing I witnessed, the more I wanted everyone healed! So, I sought God and began to grow in my understanding of His heart for wholeness for each person. I asked Him to give me His heart for others. His heart is for everyone to be healed and to walk in the identity and destiny He has created for them.

Years later, God is still showing me His best for each person. While speaking at a conference, I received several words of knowledge; one specific word was suicide. I felt prompted to give all the words of knowledge except that one. When I had finished I invited people up for prayer. A woman came up sobbing and said, "I was going to commit suicide, but God told me to come here today." In an instant, I threw my arms around her and hugged her for a time. Then, I showed her my notes where suicide was listed with my words of knowledge. I told her. "God knew you would come and He prepared this time to get rid of all those thoughts of suicide." After praying, the spirit of suicide left her and she felt free. Later, she shared how she had struggled with suicidal thoughts for many years.

Did you know emotional wounding could be a source of physical illness? A lady referred to us by another pastor believed her life had gone on hold since the murder of her daughter six years back. The fact the police and the FBI were unable to make an arrest in the case due to lack of evidence had taken an emotional toll on her and her family. Her life as she knew it had come to a halt. No longer did she enjoy being home – especially alone. She had become tired of being constantly on the go just to avoid being home. What she didn't reveal in the beginning was that she had been experiencing a sharp pain in her stomach since the night of her daughter's murder. Our prayer session was pretty typical. The Holy Spirit revealed the lies she believed as well as the guilt she clutched along with her anger over the loss of her daughter and the inability to bring her daughter's murderer to justice. It was amazing to watch as she was given truth to replace the lies; her guilt was relieved and her anger was abated.

But wait, there is more! Two months later, she made another appointment. We thought she was coming for more healing. As it turned out, she was coming to give testimony about what had happened since our last session. She was now able to enjoy being home. And for the first time in six years, she had cooked Thanksgiving dinner, making meals for her neighbors who were shut-ins. And there is more! When she concluded, I asked if there was anything we could pray about and she told us of the sharp pain she had in her stomach. We began to pray, commanding the pain to loosen, and it left! God set her free and made her whole. Praise God! Praise God! One closing note, a few days later I was ministering at a meeting and she was there. I asked how the pain was in her stomach and she replied, "It is gone and I have forgotten all about it!"

God Is Speaking

Can you hear him? If you are saved, you have heard Him! It is how you got saved. He is the Voice that called, and you responded with "yes!"

147

Hearing comes in so many ways. When I say hearing, I am not limiting it to an audible sound. I am speaking about that small inner voice that gently guides you. Or the times when you are reading and the words jump off the page; this is God speaking to you. You can sense God's communication through your thoughts, images in your mind, numbers, colors, fragrances, experiencing a cool breeze where there is none or warmth that comes over you for no explainable reason. Other times you feel a nudge to do something that is out of your wheelhouse. (I often feel the urge to call a specific person, but my first reaction is WHY? I have no understanding as to why I would call, but I am nudged to do it. In my obedience, to my amazement, God has prepared the opportunity for me to bring encouragement to them or for them to have encouragement for me; most of the time, it is mutually beneficial.)

Hearing God through others can be a wonderful surprise. It is truly special, because you realize you are so important to Him that He would send another person to tell you. It is like a kiss from God, even when He brings a word of correction. A correction from God should make you feel loved. If it does not, go back to the Lord and ask if the correction was really from Him. His audible voice is yet another way of hearing from God. God is always talking in these ways and in others through His Spirit that lives in us.

When we pray for healing with others we often find rapid healing comes if the person is able to hear directly from God. We have also found many do not believe they can hear God. And frankly, that is the lie of the enemy. Everyone can hear from God – everyone! We have exercises we do with those who are struggling from Jennifer Toledo's book, *Eyes that see and Ears that hear.*

One goes like this. Try it for yourself.

There is only one rule: you cannot allow yourself to think that it is you. We are asking to hear from God, so we trust He we will.

- Ask God to help you hear from Him.
- Ask God, if He could play any game with you, what would it be?
- Write down what comes to mind.
- Now ask God why He picked that game.
- Write down what you heard.
- Look at what you have written; this was God answering your questions.
- You just heard from God.[25]

This may seem silly, but it breaks down the barriers along with removing preconceptions and gives them permission to encounter the Lord through a non-threatening conversation.

Sometimes, we do not recognize God or the way He communicates with us, and we need a little help in connecting. Believing you cannot hear from God occupies space that actually belongs to the Lord. As we exercise our ability to hear from God, our communications with Him becomes free to flow.

Essential Oils and Frequencies

God has released insights regarding the use of leaves and plants for medicines and oils to bring healing to our bodies, just as He has given great insights to the healing power of certain

---

25 Toledo, Jennifer, *Eyes that see & Ears that hear: A Parent's Guide to Teaching Their Children How to Hear the Voice of God*, (Dinuba, Global Children's Movement, 2007), 18.

sound frequencies. Many doctors have begun to utilize prayer, oils, and frequencies along with medicine in their practice of healing. Through my own research and experimentation, I have found essential oils and frequencies to be a great addition to physical, emotional and spiritual wholeness. The results were so powerful that I incorporated them in my own life; finding relief for migraines, muscle pain and sinus congestion.

We now use both essential oils and frequencies in our Healing and Encounter Rooms. There are many books on the subject, however the two I have read are *Healing Oils of the Bible* by David Stewart and *The Physics of Heaven* by Judy Franklin and Ellyn Davis. We have also purchased the CD package called "Wholetones" by Michael Tyrrell about the healing properties of sound frequencies. These resources are a good place to start for those who are interested in learning more.

Below is an excerpt from Michael Tyrrell's website on the different frequencies and their benefits. [26]

"Simply by listening daily to this music you could...

1. **Wipe out** your unhealthy fears, drop feelings of guilt and shame, and show you how you can help restore your liver, brain, and kidney functions...(SONG 1, 396Hz)

2. **Remove** the recurring, negative cycles in your life like procrastination, addiction, and junk food...watch as sluggishness and lethargy disappear and productivity and creativity increase... enhance your digestion, ease stomach issues, balance your metabolism, and erase headaches and lower back pain... (SONG 2, 417Hz)

26 Wholetones: Healing Fequency Music Project, wholetones.com

3. Discover the Master Key that precipitates all other frequencies. You'll feel soothed by its multiple health benefits as you're tenderly enveloped in peace. This is the very same frequency David used to soothe King Saul's depression... (SONG 3, 444Hz)

4. Hear the most curious frequency of all... it has the power to relax you... transform your stress into peaceful bliss. Creating the ideal environment for your body to repair hormonal imbalances, ease muscle tension, and release troubles of circulation... (SONG 4, 528Hz)

5. Enjoy the fostering of peace and forgiveness in all your relationships. Also known to positively affect the endocrine system – particularly gall bladder and adrenal issues...(SONG 5, 639Hz)

6. Gain a keen awareness of your very own spirit in this powerful yet delicately performed miracle of healing. Experience deep spiritual and emotional healing while cleansing your immune system of common infections. Super-charge your circulatory system to support your healthy heart and blood flow...(SONG 6, 741Hz)

7. Revel in the frequency that celebrates the King of Kings. Purely spiritual – connect in the worship of God, His love for humankind, and His return to those who await Him... (SONG 7, 852Hz)"

Here is Chelsea's amazing testimony of healing through prayer, essential oils and diet.

I had battled chronic fatigue and random rashes with joint pains for years. It was in September of 2009 that months of medical testing, rounds of office visits with multiple specialists all culminated in the diagnosis: systemic lupus and possible relapsing remitting multiple sclerosis. It was hard coming to terms with the fact I had a life-altering illness, yet it was a relief to know what was plaguing my body. I sank into a depression.

Over the next three years, I packed on weight, gaining forty pounds from the steroids. Having had periodic blood draws, my numbers continued to deteriorate until I saw a rheumatologist in August 2012. He shook his head as he reviewed the numbers and said, "This is the worst set of numbers I've seen since I diagnosed you three years ago! I don't know what you are doing, but if you don't make serious life changes, you are going to parent your children from a wheelchair." Through gritted teeth, I told him I was going to heal myself from the inside out and he would never speak sickness over me again! He laughed, but said, "It's people like you that usually do get well. Good luck!" Challenge accepted! I decided at that moment to take control of my health. The first thing I needed to do was get control of my weight that had been spiraling out of control. I had ballooned up to two hundred twenty-two pounds. This was going to be a challenge because I did not believe what I ate had any effect on my health in terms of my autoimmune disorder.

So, I started reading a book on anti-inflammatory diets, and I began a diet with supplements immediately. I was stunned when I lost sixteen pounds in a short time. I was so encouraged that I just had to stick with it this time. God helped me overcome a lot during this period of my life. I learned to start viewing food as fuel, not comfort. God also helped me to break free of the bondages of emotional eating. When I saw the doctor again in November, he was pleased that I was making progress and told me to stay with it. I was feeling better.

I had learned of essential oils in December 2012, but I never asked if they could help the lupus until April 2013. I knew I did not want to keep taking the medication, anti-inflammatories and steroids, so I did my research, talked to my doctor, and prayed. Then, I decided to make the switch. I began using essential oils topically over certain organs to bring restoration and I added some as daily supplements. I even found it beneficial to diffuse specific essential oils in both my office and in my home. I prayed a lot; I even would take the labels off my water bottles and replace them with labels I had made that said HEALING WATER. When I would pick up the bottle to drink, I would tell myself I was drinking healing water. Faith comes by hearing y'all – just saying!

In October 2013, I saw the rheumatologist who sat stunned before me. I had lost ninety pounds. I had gone from a BMI (body mass index) of 41% down to 22%. I had been a size twenty-two and was now a size six! I had blood work three times where all my numbers had come back in the normal range with no markers out of range! The doctor cleared me medically. He said, "I am cutting you loose because you no longer require the care of a specialist. You call me if you feel like you need to see me and keep up the tremendous work."

I hugged him good-bye and have not seen him since. I am down ninety pounds. I am still pain-free and symptom-free. I continue to use my oils. I continue on my path of wellness. And I am walking in divine health! For me, I believe it was a combination of things: prayer, clean and healthy eating, the use of essential oils and the best healer I know, Poppa God! God gave us everything we need for health and wholeness when He created this earth, including essential oils for our medicine! – *Chelsea*

Physical Well-Being

I mentioned earlier how my desperation for healing was the result of my mom's passing away at the age of 59. My life became centered on learning how to heal others the way Jesus healed. One of the first things I realized was here on earth not everyone gets healed and for a time that was part of my wrestling. Why, Lord? I had even heard of the top ten reasons people were not healed. Then I realized, I was not only asking the wrong question, but my focus was wrong as well.

My focus should have been on the Word of God and on what God says about healing. I came to realize I am to release God's love with every healing I pray and let God be the Healer. I made a decision, regardless of what my experience was or how dire the circumstances were, I was going after healing for anyone who wanted it.

Do you remember Sears Christmas catalog? It would come in the mail and be filled with every toy imaginable. We would look through it, mark what each of us wanted, dog-earring each page. This is how I am about healing. I feel like I am a little girl at Christmas asking God for my Christmas list:

I want healing for Autism, Cancer, and Lung diseases.

Mental illness, Multiple sclerosis, Muscular Dystrophy, Myasthenia Gravis, and many others!

Lord, I want everyone healed!

Reading the healing accounts over and over in the Word only fuels me with expectancy! I hear the testimonies of healing, and I look to the Lord saying, "That's awesome. Now give me the breakthrough, Lord. Give us greater breakthroughs!" I long for healing to flow as easily as it did from Jesus, and frankly, I want everyone supernaturally healed!

At The Gathering Apostolic Center, we have a Testimony Wall with many amazing reports of healing. Everyone can read the amazing things God has done and be encouraged. Here are just a few to boost your faith and jumpstart your healing.

- My left hip was higher than my right, but after prayer, my hips aligned.

- Arthritis pain has been strong – team prayed and the pain left.

- My doctor diagnosed me as insulin-resistant. The team prayed for several months, and when I was retested, there were no indicators of being insulin-resistant.

- I had prayer for my uneven hip. While they prayed, I felt my shorter leg grow, and my stance became balanced as my leg grew.

- I was healed of flu-like symptoms after attending Healing Rooms.

- I was healed of sciatica after prayer.

- I had a migraine and after having prayer, it was gone!

- Gentleman barely able to walk on metal crutches and in great pain left waving his crutches over his head and no more pain!

God uses many resources to heal our bodies: doctors, medicines, exercise and the supernatural. I have heard Pastor Bill Johnson say, "There is no second-class healing!"

If God uses a doctor, Praise God!

If God uses the miraculous, Praise God!

If God uses our better stewardship, Praise God!

My passion, and I hope it is yours too, is to keep going after the Moses Principle—our eyes will not lose sight and our bodies will not lose strength! And God Himself will have to come and take us out! Amen? AMEN!

Perfect health comes in the Name of Jesus.

"And on the basis of faith in His name, it is the name of Jesus which has strengthened this man whom you see and know; and the faith which comes through Him has given him this perfect health in the presence of you all" (Acts 3:16 NASB).

God desires us to be healthy physically, spiritually, and emotionally. In these last two chapters, we have covered much ground for you to prayerfully consider and test for yourself.

Digging Deeper:

I have covered two different aspects of healing: emotional and physical.

- List areas you need healing.

- Pray through each item on the list asking the Holy Spirit what course of action you need to take. Remember, you might not hear something immediately. Sometimes, the Lord will highlight something as you go.

- Ask the Lord if it is time to have an emotional checkup.

- List areas you have been healed.

- This is your testimony; review it often to build your faith.

"Beloved, I pray that you may prosper in all things and be in health, just as your soul prospers" (3 John 1:2 NKJV).

Chapter 9

POSITIONING FOR HIS ALL

"Don't just learn from God's Word, but believe it will change your life." —Joyce Meyer[27]

---

27 https://www.goodreads.com/author/quotes/8352.Joyce_Meyer? page=2 (accessed 10.121.7)

A few years ago, God have me a series to preach on Sundays called *Living out of the Ease of Heaven*. We began to see God move on our behalf from this series as it changed our perspective on what is available from Heaven. We grew together as we encountered the Lord and replaced our old way of thinking with the truth of God. The Word of God came alive! We activated His Word and experienced God through tangible evidence in our lives by putting into action the principles we learned to receive God's all for our needs.

At the Gathering with Jesus at our Apostolic Center we continue to pursue living out of Heaven's abundance intended for our lives. Each week during our Sunday service, we have a time for testimonies.

One of our couples testified several weeks in a row how God had provided checks in the mail, opportunities to work, unexpected refunds and the gift of a car – a car! We also had a testimony from a single mom who was given a scholarship for college that was normally allocated to freshmen, and she was a junior!

We have tangible evidence through the people sitting in the chairs next to us that builds our faith every time we meet. This encourages us to go after God to do it again in our own area of need. We know when one has a breakthrough it opens the door for others to receive their breakthrough. We continue Sunday after Sunday celebrating God moving on behalf of our family!

The Lord tells us He is "...abounding in goodness..." (Exodus 34:6 NKJV). The word abounding means abundance, more than enough, exceedingly. God is the God of abundance in every aspect of who He is. He is more than enough, exceedingly more, in all His children's needs. This is a truth that needs to permeate our very core. We have a good God living inside of us. He tells us to:

"Ask and it will be given to you; seek and you will find; knock and the door will be opened to you....how much more will your heavenly Father give the Holy Spirit to those who ask Him!" (Luke 11:9, 13 NKJV)

The Holy Spirit is the Father's gift of Oneness to us through His Son Jesus Christ. We ask and we receive; we seek and we find what we are looking for. We knock, and doors are opened for us to move forward. God gives us practical examples of how this works in our lives. God "...anointed Jesus with the Holy Spirit and with power, who went about doing good and healing all who were oppressed by the devil, for God was with Him" (Acts 10:38 NKJV).

Notice how the triune God functions together. God the Father anointed Jesus with the Holy Spirit. Theirs is a fluid movement of Oneness. We carry this same Oneness with the Father, Son and Holy Spirit to release the goodness of God and to live in His abundant love, healing, and prosperity. All because the triune God is with us! And if God is in us, then His *all* is available to us. Do you see how these truths apply to your life?

Carriers of His Glory

Now think of yourself as a carrier of His Glory. I do not always think of myself that way, as a carrier of the glory, but I am. Jesus says you are! During one of His most intimate conversations with His Father, Jesus says,

"And the glory which You gave Me I have given them, that they may be one just as We are one" (John 17:22 NKJV).

We are carriers of God's glory or *doxa* in Greek. It means the radiance, the splendor of God. Is that not amazing? We carry the radiance – the splendor of God.

On many occasions while writing this book, I would stop and just begin to worship.

"God, how I love You; You are so majestic, You are beautiful. You are my creator, You are my provider."

And as I spoke I would become overwhelmed with His glory. Sometimes, it came like a wind swirling around me. Sometimes, a tingling began in my hands while other times warmth encased me. At times, I even felt an incredible acceptance and a sense of closeness to His holiness – to HIS GLORY!

God is drawn to our praise and our worship. We are created for worship! When we are thanking Him for all the things He has done, the glory He has given us attracts His greater glory. Suddenly, we are encased and surrounded by the amazing glory of God. Try it for yourself and experience the beauty of God's goodness, His abounding love, and let His glory overtake you. You are a carrier of His goodness, a carrier of His abundance and of His everlasting love – of His glory!

Closing the Gap between Heaven and Earth

One of the things that is necessary for us to do is to take the knowledge we have about God in our minds and begin to practice it in our daily lives. By doing this, we close the gap between Heaven and Earth. We literally pull down Heaven into our reality; and as we call the unseen into the visible it brings His abundance. Here is an example of putting what we know about God into practice and the testimony that came from it.

> I was visiting an office for treatment and during the session the therapist mentioned a pain in her back that she had for many years. Immediately, I laid my hands on the location of the pain and called everything back into order. I declared there was no pain in Heaven and sent it to the Cross. I commanded the muscles to relax, allowing everything to be ordered by God. I released peace over her back and blessed her. The next time I saw her she said her back was better, and she thanks God every night for it! – *Peggy*

Did you catch it? HIS WORLD INVADING OURS! Often, we are centered on the healing alone when we need to consider the *domino effect* healing creates. In this case, every night when she praises God, she will experience His Presence, which will bring her in a more intimate relationship with the Lord. When we thank God every night, it opens our heart for a deeper relationship with Him, which brings change to us. This opens the possibility for her family to be changed. A healing is never just a healing; God does so much more than we see or recognize. Much like dominos lined up and falling over one after another, one Heavenly event can be the catalyst for others to take place – creating the DOMINO EFFECT!

In reading this book I trust you have learned and gained revelation with understanding. Do not stop at the acquisition of knowledge! Be intentional and take the steps needed to put each revelation into practice. I have heard Bill Johnson say many times and I paraphrase: *If we do not let out what God has put in us, it will die.* In a practical application, think about all the things you learned during your school years. There are things you learned that you use regularly, for example, Math. You use it every day, in simple ways like counting how many hours until you leave work or pick up the kids. The more you use math or the more you let it out, the more your proficiency increases. But, then there were things I learned like Spanish that died because I did not let it out or put it in to practice. Can you relate? To be fully immersed in God's dreams and plans for us, we must practice at every opportunity. The more we practice, the more in-sync with God we become. With God it is not a one-shot deal,

Putting into practice what we have learned closes the gap between Heaven and Earth. This can be risky, because we are experimenting with something new. However, the more we risk (practice) each day releasing all that God has placed inside us, the more we develop a Oneness with God.

This is a great testimony of releasing God's Presence.

I went away to finish the rewrites on this book. The place I was staying had a spa, so I decided to have a facial. As the esthetician put a mask on my face I became distracted by the weird music that was playing in the background. It was really beginning to bother me. So, I decided to release the Presence of Jesus in the atmosphere. I began to pray silently and suddenly, with my eyes closed, I saw Jesus hovering close to the ceiling. He began to talk to me about things I had been pondering. Then, I realized the music had stopped and I asked the esthetician what happened to the music – she didn't know. Not only did God surprise me with His Presence, He stopped the irritating music.

Positioned for the Impossible

We are positioned for the impossible every day! This seems like a dramatic statement; nevertheless, it is true. Just as Jesus went around doing good, healing the sick, defeating the enemy, multiplying food, so can we! We align ourselves with Him, positioning ourselves for the unexpected and practicing the release of what He gives us. There are several ways to grow in our positioning with the Lord that we may co-labor in releasing the impossible.

Develop a Working Knowledge of Him with You

This working knowledge comes from spending time alone with God and learning how He connects with you personally. There are many facets to this, and they grow and expand as your relationship develops and matures with Him. As you spend time with God, begin to take note of the ways He connects with you though your senses: sight, touch, smell, taste and hearing.

I will share a few examples of how God connects with us through our senses.

I am a visual person, so many times; the Lord will talk to me in words, pictures or visions. As I read Scripture, often a movie begins to play in my mind or I get images showing me an understanding of the passage. Whether it is a literal meaning, a prophetic understanding or a specific detail He wants me to grasp, He connects with me through my sense of sight.

Another way He connects with me to get my attention is by giving me a tingling sensation in my fingers. It is an indication He is Present and ready to move.

I was invited to preach and minister at a Friday night service and during worship, I moved to the back of the room to get a bigger picture of what was happening. Suddenly, I felt God's Presence drop into the room. I asked God what He wanted to do and He responded, "You do what you want to do, and I will cover it." I had felt the tingling in my hands and I knew it was time for healing to be released. As soon as I realized it I was called to the front and the pastor whispered, "Do whatever is on your heart. No restraint. No time limit." God released healing in a mighty way that night, specifically in joints, necks, shoulders and backs! Amazing!

Another example of encountering God through our senses is a sudden unexplainable fragrance in the air.

A teenage boy came to me after service and told me how he suddenly smelled a sweet perfume during worship. He began to look around to find out who was applying perfume during the service and could find no one. He realized it was Jesus surrounding him with a sweet fragrance of His presence!

Many, including myself, have been saturated by His fragrance as a manifestation of His Presence. When working in my home office, I am frequently overwhelmed by the smell of the different aromas that are not naturally there: scents of vanilla, roses and peppermint, to name a few.

Here is a testimony of God communicating through the sense of hearing.

Driving home from work, I had to travel through a particularly dangerous part of the highway. I would always slow down and become a little anxious before entering what people referred to as Death Valley. One time the drive home was especially tense. Traffic was bumper-to-bumper, cars pulling on the highway, while others attempted to make left turns from the fast lane. It was a sea of taillights in chaos. I slowed down, dropping into fourth gear, when suddenly, I heard a voice speak; "I am with you, I will never abandon you, I will never leave you." His voice was as plain as someone sitting behind me. I glanced to the back and there was Jesus sitting in the backseat of my car! Immediately, my anxiety left and I drove home without incident. To this day when I drive, I look for Jesus in the car and if I do not see Him, I say, "I know You are here; show Me where You are." – *Diane*

"All You have, Lord!"

I have spent many years seeking an intimate relationship with the Lord and have gone through seasons of saturation and seasons of dryness. For a year I spent every available moment crying out to God. I read His Word and other books about Him. I also spent time with people who had deeper relationships with God, doing whatever ever it took to ENCOUNTER GOD! Frankly, the last twenty-plus years have been of the same intensity. The more He gives me, the more I want to know. I tell Him all the time, "I want all You have and I want it now." With the more He gives me, the more I want EVERYONE to know and encounter Him.

This pursuit of intimacy is for you. You want all of God and all He has promised! God promises that if we draw near to Him, He will draw near to us. As we seek Him, we will find Him. It is His desire and His dream for us to experience the awe and wonder of having an intimate, beautiful relationship with Him!

Learning to Love – LOVE Beyond Our Knowledge

Scripture says that without love, we are nothing. Every word Jesus spoke and every action Jesus took was out of love because He is love. His love for us is tender... His love is accepting... His love stirs beauty from deep inside of us ... His love makes us feel secure.... His love makes us want to be **the** best we can be. His love is forever and ever. When we operate out of love, all of Heaven responds, because it recognizes the Father's heart beating in you.

We have a Bible college that is in partnership with our school, *the Gathering School of Supernatural Activation.* Together we offer accredited degrees. Our first six-week course is *Loving Beyond the Knowledge.* We learn that God loves us beyond the knowledge He has of us. This means He loves us even though He knows everything about us. He wants us to learn how to love others in the same way. To love beyond what we know and perceive of them. God wants to reveal the hidden treasure in each of us: the gold. He wants us to take the time to mine the gold and bring it to the surface, visible for all to see the fullness of who God created us to be; it is called *Digging for the Gold*!

When we are able to see the gold in others and love them while the gold is rising to the surface, then we have loved like God loves. Remember reading in John 4 about Jesus encountering the Samaritan woman at the well? Jesus knew all about her; she had five husbands and the one she was living with was not even one of them. Jesus did not focus on her past or her sin. His focus was to lead her to truth and to the Father's plan for her. Her future was lived out of Jesus's love and His complete acceptance of her.

This is our challenge: to be able to love others, not distancing ourselves or judging them and not losing sight of the future the Father has for them. This is why we should listen when others receive prophecy. This way we will know how God sees and describes them so we can treat them in that way. "Walking in love that passes knowledge brings God's perfected love and the fullness of God into our lives. This gives us the ability to be led by the Father as Jesus was."[28]

Walking in Unfettered Obedience

According to *Merriam-Webster*, the word "unfettered" means unrestrained, unrestricted, unbridled, uninhibited. If you remove the prefix "un" from every word listed, then we see the restrictions that hold us back. We live in a world of restraint for multiple reasons; fear is the biggest. We have fear of failing, fear of over-stepping our boundaries in talking about Jesus, or fear of offending someone with our speech.

Unbelief can be the greatest restraint. We genuinely cannot bring ourselves to believe the kind of love, the kind of freedom and the kind of abundance God has for us. We miss the fullness of what God wants to do in us and through us by hesitating in following His lead.

On the other hand, being unfettered, unrestrained, and unbridled in our obedience to God gives us a life filled with

28 (Dr. Tony Slay, Ministry International Institute Year One, P12).

adventure! When you wake up saying to the Lord, "I am available for whatever You have planned!" then you are willing to take the risk of putting into practice what you have learned. It is amazing to see people come alive when they have received the love of Christ pouring out of you.

Every month we have treasure hunts at the Gathering Apostolic Center where we go out and look for the gold in others.

One particular time, the team prayed at the police station and continued with a prayer walk in the surrounding area. They knocked on doors and offered prayer as the Holy Spirit nudged. They stopped at a laundromat and had the opportunity to pray and prophesy over a young woman. It was a wonderful time of following God to places He had prepared.

Think about the DOMINO EFFECT of just that one day! We have an invitation to do this every day. God will guide us as we go for encounters that will touch others.

I know for me, when God first started nudging me to approach strangers, it was hard.

On one occasion I was running in the park, and I saw a lady with a cane sitting on a bench. Immediately, I felt a nudge to go and pray with her, but I decided to keep running. The intensity to go back was so strong; I finally turned around and asked if I could join her. Of course, I thought she needed prayer for her knees since she used a cane. When I asked if I could pray for her, she said she didn't really need anything, but I could pray if I wanted to. As I started to pray God began to speak to me about her daughter, so that is what I prayed. Sure enough, she was concerned about her daughter and appreciated the prayer!

In the times I have approached people to pray for them, I only have had a few people tell me no. God sends us to those who need to feel His love. Are you ready to release His love?

Testify, Testify, Testify!

I mentioned earlier that each Sunday morning, we have a time of testimony, giving the opportunity to others to share what the Lord has done in their life that week. It is amazing to hear what is shared. We celebrate what God has done in our church families' lives during the past week. Sometimes, He has not finished the work, but we celebrate what He has already done and we celebrate any incremental change. Here are two testimonies: one when healing came incrementally and another when healing was completed instantaneously.

In 2003, I went to Taiwan as part of a team to teach on prayer, healing and deliverance. One of the leaders was a young pastor named Charity Chen. She had been afflicted with polio as a small child and she needed metal braces and forearm crutches to walk. In 1986, during a time of healing prayer, the bones in her feet began to move, but it was not enough for her to do without the crutches or rid her of the constant pain. However, I received a newsletter awhile back and one of the articles was "Jesus Healed Me!" It was Charity's story of how she has now been completely healed. The interesting part of the article was that no one was praying for healing; they were all praying for guidance in Charity's next steps. And suddenly, her bones in her legs and feet began to move until she was completely healed and pain-free. She took off the metal braces and danced for over an hour!

Here is a recent testimony from Julie when she visited our Healing and Encounter Rooms:

I was plagued since birth with chronic lung infections, from bronchitis and pneumonia, to hacking coughs and debilitating exhaustion following each episode. Last February, after six grueling and bedridden months of suffering from one upper respiratory infection to another, I made my way to the Healing Rooms at "The Gathering with Jesus" for prayer and encouragement.

Though I could hardly stand on my own, just being there and feeling the presence of God gave me immediate nourishment; I was feeling unconditional love and peace as I always do when I am there. I approached my pastor for prayer, and she asked another to join us. They started praying over me and asked the Holy Spirit to come. They asked for wisdom. Without me saying a word, the other woman asked if she could put her hands on me and on my lungs, and the pastor told me that she saw a vision of "perfect lungs" suspended over me – lungs! Pink, healthy and vibrant lungs! The other woman said there was a storeroom in heaven into which we can reach, and the pastor said she felt the Lord was directing her to "install" these lungs in me! They proceeded to pray in the Spirit, and we all felt an incredible heat and swirling movement go through us. We held on to each other as Heaven worked. As I opened my eyes, Pastor Cindy asked me to take a deep breath. Normally, I would be hesitant because it would cause me to start coughing in close proximity to someone, but I breathed in because I knew Jesus had touched me. Wow! Amazed, I breathed in again—a long, hard, deep breath.

No coughing, No crackling, No pain, just breath! A total miracle! I breathed so much that I got dizzy and had to sit down. That was five months ago.

Since then, even when surrounded by people who are coughing or sneezing, I don't worry because my lungs are strong. I sleep with the windows open because I am no longer wheezing, no matter the season. I am swimming longer and faster because of my increased lung capacity. My lungs are brand new, healthy and strong. Thank you, Jesus! – *Julie*

Are You Ready?

Jesus has prepared so much for us to experience while we are here on Earth. And our engaging with Him makes room for His realm of Heaven to invade ours. The goal for us, as believers, is to be a unified force in breaking open God's plan for us.

We truly can be world-changers!

Digging Deeper:

With each step you take, God honors that step and joins you in the next step. He wants His Kingdom to invade Earth through His children, His heirs – you and me! So, dive in with all that you have and be positioned for His All.

- Spend time learning how God connects with you.

- Ask the Lord to demonstrate His unconditional love for you.

- Ask Him to teach you to love beyond the knowledge you have of others.

- Ask God each morning for His plans for the day.

- Write your testimony and share it with somebody.

Chapter 10

ENTER HIS LIFE OF ABUNDANCE

"The same Jesus who turned water into wine can transform your home, your life, your family, and your future. He is still in the miracle-working business, and His business is the business of transformation." —Adrian Rogers[29]

---

29 https://www.christianquotes.info/quotes-by-topic/quotes-about-trans-formation/#ixzz4vOB4zUpy (accessed 10.13.17)

My husband and I wanted our son to go to college without incurring any debt. We had planned ahead with the Florida Prepaid College Savings Program. He was a good student and a basketball player; so, with this combination, we thought we were financially set. As we visited colleges with him, it was determined God's best for our son was a private college in Boston. We knew when we walked on the campus this was the place; however, our Florida Prepaid fund would barely make a dent in the tuition. We prayed and our answer from God was to go forward. Our yes to God came with a caveat: no debt for our son or us. Over the next four years, every time tuition was due, God provided. Our son graduated, and God provided every penny we needed, over and above the $160,000 in tuition. All our son's expenses, including the car we bought for him, had all been paid. ALL PAID! God is amazing in His supply!

Abundance is not limited to our finances. Abundance is a way of life in the Kingdom of God. Throughout God's Word, there are foundational principles in how we can experience abundance in all areas: family, finances, physical and emotional wholeness.

In John 10:10, Jesus told his disciples,

"A thief has only one thing in mind: he wants to steal, kill, and destroy. But my desire is to give you everything in abundance, more than you expect—life in its fullness until you overflow!" (TPT)

We will address the role of the "thief" in a few minutes, but first we must dissect what Jesus is offering us. There are several keys found in the second half of the sentence.

Jesus's desire is to give us...

Everything in abundance

that will

exceed our expectations,

producing an

overflowing life!

Overflowing Life

God has made an overflowing life possible from the beginning. In Genesis 1:26, Adam was created – a man was created in God's image. In that creative time, he and later, Eve, were created in a body that was perfected, in an environment that was perfected with the abundance of beauty and glory surrounding them. There was an abundance of everything; they even had more than they could ever need. Above all, they were surrounded by the presence of God, who produced this overflowing life for them.

Their sin against the very presence of God and His provision of abundance created a chasm – a gaping void – between them and their ability to stay close to God. Their focus shifted from the wonder and beauty of God being the very center of their life to the external perspective that even in lavish abundance, there was lack. This is where the enemy came to kill the truth spoken into their hearts, to steal their ability to see and to destroy their intimacy with God. The twisting of God's word created a perspective that something was withheld from them that would be better than the spoken words of God.

Living in abundance comes by being permeated –soul and body – in truth, so your actions line up with God's word.

"Let me, your servant, walk in abundance of life, that I may always live to obey your truth" (Psalms 119:17 TPT).

An abundant, overflowing life comes from walking in the truth of God's word. "This commandment that I'm commanding you today isn't too much for you; it's not out of your reach. No! The word is right here and now – as near as the tongue in your mouth, as near as the heart in your chest. Just do it!" (Deuteronomy 30:11,14 MSG)

As believers in Jesus, we know the Word is no longer merely near to us, rather, He lives in us.

Jesus Is the Word... and the Word Lives in Us!

We do not need to wait for someone to come to tell us to do this or to do that. No! The Word is in us and we have access to the Word – Jesus – 24 hours a day, seven days a week – instant access! Jesus is in us. Everything we need is accessible through Him. Overflowing abundant life comes from a life centered on Jesus. He gives us a true perspective of His abundance in every aspect of our lives.

One of the devotionals I love to read is *100 Days in the Secret Place*, by Gene Edwards. It includes the classic writings by one of my favorites: Madame Guyon. She wrote that St. Augustine had said that "...he had lost so much time in the beginning of his Christian experience by trying to find the Lord outwardly rather than by turning inwardly." As we turn inward to connect our spirit with His Spirit, she explains, "As revelation comes to you, something happens: Jesus Christ actually makes an imprint of Himself upon your soul. Each time He comes to you, He leaves a new and different impression of His nature upon you."[30]

Jesus permeates our spirit, flooding us with an imprint. His presence is like a branding iron searing our hearts with the His truth. His revelation saturates our spirit and our soul and our body. It is this infusion of Him that brings our mind, heart and emotions into abundant life. Our thoughts and feelings are surrendered, healed and restored to receive the abundant life in Christ. Our bodies, every bone, every organ, every cell — every aspect is surrendered to His truth for healing and restoration, as we receive abundant life in Christ.

I have had so many things healed in my soul as well as in my physical body. The most recent was the final touch of healing of my chronic migraines and sinus issues. Previously, I had received a level of healing for this issue, and then a few months ago, there was a sudden increase. I was traveling to Africa when my sinuses began to hurt and the migraine followed. It was then I told the Lord that this had to end. The conference I was speaking at was important and I could not battle this any longer. The interesting thing was I didn't have any problems while I was there, but I didn't notice I was healed until I came home. We had a flurry of

---

30 Edwards, Gene, *100 days in the Secret Place: Classic Writings From Madame Guyon, Francois Fenelon, & Michael Molinos on the Deeper Christian Life*, (Shippensburg: Destiny Image Publishing, 2015), 208, 211.

hurricanes when I returned, which in the past would immediately trigger a migraine and sinus problems, but this time it didn't! Not one migraine, not one sinus complication. A migraine tried to sneak in later, but I reminded my body that God had taken care of this issue, and it did not last! I was healed!

Jesus is transforming our lives from glory to glory, just like He did with Moses. We are continually being permeated from the inside out by the radiance of God's glory! Our obedience to the words of God, our life surrendering to intimacy, produces the exceedingly, abundantly, overflowing life!

Pattern for Abundance

It is in an atmosphere of success that we choose to enter in through our obedience, and the abundance of the success is inter-dependent on our intimacy with God. Like many of you, I have spent years trying to understand what success is in the eyes of God.

In the Book of Joshua chapter one, the Lord gave two specific instructions in how to ensure success. Feast on the Word until your heart is strong and your mind is renewed, obeying the Lord at all cost. Joshua followed this direction, and as a result, he had success in all he did and prospered. It comes across simple enough, but the daily implementation is a little more challenging.

The Lord never meant His abundance to benefit only one person. From God's perspective, the prospering of one has a radiating effect on others within our family and within the community in which we live. We do not live with a dependence on others for abundance. God has planned for each of us to be an outpouring of abundance to one another, as demonstrated with Joshua. His obedience brought success, and everyone benefited.

Our Apostolic Center was in need of a custodian. When our leadership team discussed it, everyone thought of the same person for the job. Later, when we called the person, they related they had been praying for extra income and knew this was an answer to their prayers. They were excited to start.

Abundant Life Produces Love

The very core of our life in Jesus is birthed from Love. There is a simplicity held within His Word from which a fluid theme flows from every page: LOVE. And, found within that love of God runs the river of abundance. This abundance is the fruit of love.

"And the Lord your God will circumcise your heart and the heart of your descendants, to love the Lord your God with all your heart and with all your soul, that you may live" (Deuteronomy 30:6 NKJV).

The Lord provided a way to love by the tenderness of His hands cutting the callus from our heart and replacing it with a soft supple capacity to love. Imagine, He pours His love over our tough, hardened, love-resistant heart. Softening our hearts with His oil of extravagant love, he washes away all that hinders us from loving the way He does.

His love permeates the core of our emotions and brings healing so we can live. We received the revelation of the Father's love for us through Jesus. We experience this supernatural love poured into our spirit.

Living out of His love means letting go of everything that does not carry love. Hurt, self-hatred, insecurity, shame, humiliation, abuse, anger, un-forgiveness —- all of these and more are the plan of the enemy to destroy us. But the enemy's plan will not work because the love of Jesus heals and removes all of these things.

God gave me a word about humiliation and how it stunts our ability to move into His purposes. I remember the story of a young woman who came in because she struggled with being able to move forward in the way she wanted. The Lord showed her how it stemmed from her youth when she was humiliated at a neighborhood cookout by her father. She had tried on her sister's makeup and when she came out, her father yelled at her, saying she looked like a hooker, and she had better get inside and wash her face. Later, as a young woman, the Lord showered her with His love. And through His love, she felt released to forgive her father and receive God's healing and the gift of confidence.

God's love is greater, more powerful than any plan the enemy can devise!

With God's heart of love, we are freed to love Him. We do this through our oneness with Him; growing in our awareness of Him, loving what He loves, while partnering with His plans. Loving Him with abandonment increases our capacity to freely love others. Loving Him with abandonment changes our view of abundance. Jesus becomes our filter so we are able to see abundance in all things.

I had a vision in 1999: I saw believers gathered together worshiping God with such great love that His Presence became dazzling and so brilliant it emanated from the place of worship to the surrounding areas, causing those in cars to pull off the highway and others to come running into the building, all being drawn by His resplendent love! They were encountering Jesus, being healed, and finding their purpose by His presence. They were experiencing His abundant love for them. His love far exceeded their expectations.

This has been my central focus since then. With each meeting I am participating in, whether at my home church or at a conference, my focus is bringing everyone into an encounter with Jesus. Every encounter with Him brings us into a greater closeness. Every encounter brings us revelation. Each encounter transforms us!

Partnering with God in Obedience Produces Abundance

Our partnership with God requires immediate obedience to Him. "And all these blessings shall come upon you and overtake you, because you obey the voice of the Lord your God" (Deuteronomy 28:2 NKJV). You can read all the blessings in Deuteronomy 28.

Sometimes, we think following God's instructions is like taking dictation: He speaks and we act. However, Joshua shows us how his alignment with God's plan gave him a voice in determining the process.

During the fight against the five kings, the same battle where God threw hailstones, Joshua needed more daylight to defeat the enemy. "Then Joshua spoke to the Lord...and he said in the sight of Israel: 'Sun, stand still over Gibeon; and Moon, in the Valley of Aijalon.' So the sun stood still, And the moon stopped, Till the people had revenge Upon their enemies" (Joshua 10:12-13 NKJV).

God delights in our obedience, rewarding us with blessings; and as we obey, we move into a deeper partnership. Joshua walked to such an extent in partnership with God that the Lord listened to the voice of a man and responded to his decree.

"Sun, stand still over Gibeon, and Moon, in the Valley of Aijalon" (ibid).

You too, can be in partnership with God. Your obedience gives you greater access to God's solutions for your problems.

This is a testimony of obedience and blessing from Sharon who attended one of our three-day conferences.

Before the conference began, I was interceding for the day. told me that if I would not join in, but rather continue my intercession during the entire conference, He would have a gift for me at the end of the three-day meeting. So, every day I arrived early and stayed after the meetings and prayed, as God would lead. During the meetings, I never sat down; I prayed pacing back and forth at the doors. On the third day, the leader was closing with an offering of communion. When God told me to go and take communion in proxy for my oldest son, I thought that was my gift, thinking it would somehow bring him to the Lord, since he was not a believer. I was so excited to see what God would do. Nine months later, my son and his wife delivered their first baby after trying for eight years. However, it was not until several months later that God revealed to me the true gift: my grandchild had been conceived the weekend of the conference! – *Sharon*

God Blesses Our Obedience with Abundance

"According to the word of the Lord, they gave him the city which he asked for...and he built the city and dwelt in it" (Joshua 19:50 NKJV).

Joshua was given what he had asked and according to research, it is the same location where he commanded the sun to stand still. Isn't that interesting? God blessed Joshua by giving him a resting place in that same region where he had victory. The Lord married the miraculous with the natural for victory over the enemy! What an outrageous God! Earlier in his life, God had forgiven Joshua for his disobedience in covenanting with the Gibeonites (see Joshua 9). He then gave Joshua the victory over that same land where He caused the sun to stand still so Joshua had time to win to the battle. And if that wasn't enough, as a crescendo, God blessed Joshua with the city of Gibeon as his inheritance. How incredible is that? God brought Joshua full circle.

God Keeps His Promises to His people

To me, this is the most remarkable piece we have explored throughout this book.

"So the Lord gave the people all the land he had promised their ancestors. The people took the land and lived there. The Lord gave them peace on all sides, as he had promised their ancestors. None of their enemies defeated them; the Lord handed all their enemies over to them. He kept every promise he had made to the Israelites; each one came true" (Joshua 21:43-45 NCV).

Not only did they receive the physical land, God also gave them peace on all sides. The enemy's plan was stopped!

Despite all our disobedience, allowing ourselves to be deceived by the enemy and excluding God from our decisions, He is still good! This is who our God is. He is a keeper of His promises and a protector of His people. And we have been invited to live in the abundance of His Promises!

Abundance Is Found in What We Possess

In 2 Kings 4, there is an account of a widow and her sons who are a part of God's family. Her husband had been a prophet in the company of prophets of Israel. When Elisha arrives, her sons are about to be taken by their creditors as slaves to pay off their debt. Elisha inquires, "...Tell me what you have in the house?" (2 Kings 4:2 NKJV) Her only possession was a jar of oil. He then instructs her to borrow jars from all the neighbors, everywhere, not just a few. Does this make any sense to you? If you were the widow and this was your son, the thought would be running through your head: how are empty jars going to help? Regardless, they do it anyway and follow his instructions going to all the neighbors. They collect the jars, bring them home and shut the door behind them. Then the miracle begins. God fills jar after jar after jar until they have no more jars and the oil stops.

Sometimes, abundance comes by using what is in our possession to be multiplied – into not just enough but abundantly more than we need!

God gave me a dream several years ago about money. In the dream, the Lord was handing me seventy-seven million dollars. In the dream, I paused, hesitating to accept this large amount of money, but I finally did. The dream ended.

Although God handed me the money, it is has not yet come to pass. The Lord and I have discussed this dream many times and He has given me different revelations regarding it; one of them being that God uses numbers in representative and idiomatic ways. That is, numbers are symbolic, and they have a meaning that is different from the meaning they are expressing. The number seven is representative of completion and perfection. Numbers are seen throughout the Bible with consistency, and their spiritual significance is not always stated or obvious. With this in mind, the number seven is defined as completion, perfection by God. Multiples and doubles show intensification. So, seventy-seven is an intensification of God's perfect completion.

In the dream, God handed me the seventy-seven million dollars or a perfect amount to bring what I needed to completion. I have been given access to everything I need. Just as the woman was given the perfect amount of oil for what she needed, we too have all we need. The money does not need to be in my bank account for me to move forward. My partnership is with God, who is a good provider and when I have a need, He provides!

Here is another amazing testimony from the Gathering with Jesus.

We began meeting in our home until we needed a bigger space. A local church offered to share space with us for a year until we were on our feet. Once we were ready for our own space, our entire body went and prayed throughout the storefront where God directed us. We received a resounding YES from God. However, we needed twenty-five thousand dollars for the build-out, which we did not have. In faith, we started moving forward with the plans, and our first investment came from our landlord, who gave us three months rent-free; two months at the beginning of our lease and one at the end. The cash to pay for our build-out came in all forms, from our Gathering family, from friends and a couple of surprises in the mail. It was amazing. We did not have to incur any debt or be concerned at any time; God took care of exactly what we needed.

These testimonies represent different monetary needs, but the basis is the same: we partnered with God in every decision and He provided all we needed out of His abundance.

God Releases Abundance through a Lifestyle of Giving

One of our families experienced overwhelming abundance through giving. One Friday night we were holding a special conference, and the young mom came while her husband stayed home with their three children. As we received an offering for the speaker, Joyce felt the Lord prompt her to give five hundred dollars! This was more than their budget allowed; however, she wrote the check. Not having discussed this with her husband beforehand made for an uneasy ride home. But once she shared it with him, she was happy to find her husband was in agreement. Come Monday morning, to their surprise, the bank called and offered to refinance their house, lowering their mortgage almost five hundred dollars a month. For months, the couple had been trying to get their mortgage refinanced without success. She was obedient in giving a one-time offering of five hundred dollars. However, God gave them five hundred dollars a month for the life of the mortgage! That is abundance from obedience! And the abundance was not limited to that. Three years later while she was working on their household budget, she called the bank about their second mortgage. To her surprise, she was told it had been paid off – over $30,000 had been PAID OFF!

Notice her motivation was not, "If I give five hundred dollars, then God will take care of my refinance and pay off my second mortgage." This young mom knew the voice of God was prompting her to give and nervously she gave, knowing the strain it would put on their budget. She also knew if it was God prompting her, He would work out the budget for her. And boy, did He!

We have heard many testimonies of God's abundance through obedient giving. Nonetheless, it is not limited to waiting on God's nudge for giving; we are designed for a *lifestyle of giving*. We are called to be generous in every opportunity.

"Give, and you will receive. You will be given much. Pressed down, shaken together, and running over, it will spill into your lap. The way you give to others is the way God will give to you" (Luke 6:38 NCV).

Did you notice the abundant life Jesus gives us goes back to our relationship with Poppa God? His Word, the testimonies we hear, and our experiences remind us that God our Father has our best interest in mind, because of who He is!

I would like to end with a quick testimony about my husband, Chuck.

Many years ago, as a family we would give an offering on Sunday, but we did not tithe. A tithe means ten percent of your gross income. What we did not understand was the relational aspect to tithing. Suddenly, Chuck had a revelation about the tithe and offering and how it would bring abundance to our family. He decided to issue a challenge to God. My wonderful husband was going to try to out-give God! I laugh as I write this, but at the time, it was a solid plan. We would get paid, our tithe was determined based on that amount, and then we added a generous offering. Then, God always increased our income. So, the next time, Chuck would tithe, matching the increase, and add to it an even more generous offering. Again, God increased our income; this continued for a long season. Every time Chuck thought, okay this will out-give God; God would blast us with more income! It became a Father-son game they played!

God's Abundance Is for You

You were created to live an abundant life. This chapter is just a small glimpse of the possibilities God has prepared for the ones who love Him. As I put the finishing touches on this book, I am also readying for my son's wedding. I look on the lives of my son and his fiancée and praise God for His promise of abundant life for my family. I spent many nights praying and talking to God about my son's future wife. I continually reminded God of His promises – not that He forgets! However, I was not going to relent until I had what was promised to me and to all of us in the Word.

The Blessed Life

The best book I have read for the biblical basis of tithing is *The Blessed Life* by Robert Morris. His book takes the reader from the Old Testament through the New Testament on the subject of God's intent of offerings and tithing for His people.

There were difficult times in my contending, from girlfriends that weren't the right fit, to standing aside while he was discovering his own relationship with God. In it all, my strength was found in His presence and in His Word. God's dream for my family is to have life more abundant in Jesus.

God has dreams for you...

He dreams of you walking in your identity as His son or His daughter.

He dreams of you being His friend.

He dreams of you fulfilling your purpose.

He dreams of you being a part of His army.

He dreams of you bringing Heaven to Earth.

He dreams of you as His-story maker.

He dreams of you preparing the next generation.

He dreams of you leaving an inheritance.

He dreams of you spending eternity with Him.

He has your life in His capable hands. No matter what it may look like, the answer is found in Him. Live His dreams for your life!

"So we are convinced that every detail of our lives is continually woven together to fit into God's perfect plan of bringing good into our lives, for we are his lovers who have been called to fulfill his designed purpose" (Romans 8:28 TPT).

EPILOGUE

My Journey with Jesus

At the end of each of my books I share my story of how God swooped me up and my life was forever changed. I pray it will encourage and provoke you to relentlessly go after God! (I have already shared some of my story in the preceding pages.)

My deep love relationship with Jesus has grown through a process of pursuit and hunger. It was not established with a formula or in an instant. Although some things did happen quickly and instantly, the only real constant is God always has a way of surprising me, and I love Him for it!

My first surprise was when I was nine years old at church camp. I was in the chapel, standing against the wall on the right side, with my arms open, shaking and crying. I was filled with fear even though I knew it was Jesus's touch causing my reactions. I was so overwhelmed by His Presence; I was unable to engage in the service. I just stood there trying to figure out what to do. I could see the service and hear them inviting others forward, but I was immobilized by what was happening to me. This encounter changed the course of my life, but not as you would think.

While I was at camp, my grandfather suddenly died. Upon my return home, my salvation encounter was never revealed to my family. I spent years having a secret relationship with Jesus, knowing He was always with me, but unable to assimilate the church's view of Jesus with the Jesus I had come to know. My secret relationship was also due in part to the confusion that followed my grandfather's death. He was one of the spiritual pillars of the church and with his spiritual influence in our home now removed, what was left was my dad's animosity toward the church and my mom's "enlightened" mindset to influence my understanding of God. In all of this, I became conflicted. God was everywhere and in everything – He was in the trees, He was in the sky – as my mother professed. While my dad's animosity revealed God's need to control me and take my money.

In my confliction, I spent years searching for the Jesus I had encountered at camp. Once married, I attended church. While serving on committees, teaching VBS, and cooking spaghetti dinners, I struggled to find the real, tangible, and loving God I had met as a child. Then my life hit a crisis. My best friend, my confidante, the woman who loved me unconditionally – my mom – died at the young age of fifty-nine. To this day, I cherish and love her deeply. Mom had had her encounter with Jesus before she turned fifty and through that she became a great person of prayer She spent the last six years of her life living and traveling with us and enjoying her grandchildren. Her relationship with Jesus greatly influenced our lives. With her loss, my search intensified. I was desperate to find the truth about God as my mother had eventually come to know.

I began to search for the truth of God. So, I challenged God to prove Himself. I gave Him goals and deadlines. As a corporate executive that is what you do. I gave Him a time frame and objectives He had to meet. He had one year to show up and show me he was real or I was going to quit believing, because there was no other option. Even as I write this, I shudder now at what could have been interpreted by others as arrogance when in reality it was my desperation crying out for the Living God. I told God He had one year to show up. I would do my part, which honestly in the beginning was more formulaic than heartfelt. However, what happened next was extra-ordinary. Since God is faithful, He responded to my passionate pleas. He began to flood me with His Presence––tangible Presence! I could feel Him, I could see Him in visions, and I could hear His voice. It was as if all my senses were opened, including taste and aromas. With trances and insights, prophetic visions and words of knowledge, I was completely undone by His holiness.

I had no idea how to define this in the confines of the church. At that time, for me it was "either-or," but no coexistence. At first, my encounters were personal and then God expanded them for other people. In some encounters, He would give me words to share. I stumbled and stammered as I tried to describe to the person what God had shown me. He also showed me several people who were going to die when I didn't even know one of them was sick. That really scared me! Many times, He gave me the details of a conflict with exact information of the problem and the wisdom to speak into the situation. At one point, He sent me to pray for a pastor when I wasn't even sure how to pray. Faithfully, the Holy Spirit moved on me releasing the right words.

I was fortunate to be surrounded with a few mature believers who were instrumental in discipling me through this process. Over the years, they invested, mentored, and helped me to grow and fall deeper in love with the Lord. God has completely turned my life upside down over the past twenty-five years.

God "tricked" me into quitting my career, which I loved at the time because it gave me my identity. My work included fifty to sixty hours a week working and traveling. However, once I quit, I ended up spending four to five hours each day in His Presence. During those hours, sitting in the park by the lake, I found the Scriptures to be my lifeline--my handbook for all situations. It was as if my eyes had been veiled all those years where I only knew "rules" of God, and then suddenly, His Presence tore the veil, and I encountered the "truth" of God: His love. I became saturated with how much He loved me and so overwhelmed by how unconditional His love was that it washed away all the years of lies, which had caused the torment, uncertainty and brokenness. God taught me to journal, recording everything He reveals to me. In the beginning, I carried a notebook everywhere, but now I use my computer, and there are times I sketch my ideas on paper. It is important for me to keep His promises in the forefront, so I do not forget the abundance of what God has done for me.

I wrote my first book, Believing God and Believing His Word, from my blog, which included the discoveries I made in my encounters with God over a two-year time frame. It was a fulfillment of a promise He made that I would write and publish books.

This journey has had its share of difficulties, too. The biggest difficulty to overcome was my transition from a static relationship with God to one with a more fluid-style interaction. Not everyone understood what God was doing in my life, and who could blame them? I did not understand, either. Though I was reserved with whom I shared God's move in my life, I was still met with much resistance from those I loved and looked up to.

I was so perplexed having to have a secret life with Jesus and

His signs and wonders and His truths of the Bible. I could not understand why it was such a problem to talk about, let alone walk in. What I had to learn was that many only want God in a palatable bite. "Why don't they want all of God?" I questioned. I had finally encountered the Lord I sought for so long and could not fathom keeping Him a secret. I wanted to run away as fast as I could, but God would not let me. He called me to stay and honor the place in which He had put me, and there came a great benefit in my staying as I grew in my dependence and trust in Him.

A well-known prophet said to me as we were visiting a mutual friend, "Something had really come at you, tried to really destroy you." And it was true. But Jesus has come to destroy the works of the enemy. So, whatever the enemy tried to use to destroy me, Jesus destroyed for me!

The Lord brought me great healing in a vision, which I share below. I pray it encourages you in your journey with Jesus!

When I saw Jesus, I fell across the steps of the Throne Room, and suddenly, He was sitting on the step as I lay across His lap, totally worn down, broken, and exhausted. Leaning forward, He began to rub my back, saying, "It really is okay. I have you. You will move for Me."

It was as if He was healing all the hurt and disappointment, and the sadness and sorrow seemed to drift away as He patted my back, soothing me like a child. "Come see," He said. We both stood, and He led the way. There was lightness in our steps, joy, laughter, and fun; it was a loving time together.

Whatever came against me, Jesus conquered!

Whatever mistakes I made, Jesus covered!

Whatever needs I had, Jesus met them!

Go after God.

Allow Him to take you where He has promised.

"No promise from God is empty of power, for with God there is no such thing as impossibility" (Luke 1:37 TPT).

DR. CYNTHIA STEWART

As a kid, Cindy Stewart dreamt of becoming a superhero! She became someone who helps others find their champion within. After years of climbing the corporate ladder, serving on boards and owning her own business, she took a break to stay home with her children. She discovered two things: she was afraid of failing and afraid to dream big! Ultimately, her journey to discover her passion included physical well-being discipline, spiritual growth and healing of the soul (mind, will and emotion). An avid learner, her education is expansive; she also completed a Doctorate in Ministry.

Cindy has a passion for people and helping them to connect to their life purpose, discover their passions and live their dreams. She accomplishes this through many different avenues. She is an Itinerant Speaker and an Executive Coach. She is also the author of two other books, *Insights for an Abundant Life – Energizing Your life with God's Word* (previously titled *Believing God and Believing His Word*) and *An Invitation to Experience God's Love with 49 Days of Activations* (previously *7 Visions: A Glimpse of the Father's Heart*). Additionally, she hosts a weekly podcast, "Unleashing the Champion Within," and she writes a blog on www.cindy-stewart.com

Cindy, along with her husband, Chuck, lead The Gathering Worship Center, which is a part of The Gathering Apostolic Center in Tarpon Springs, FL. Together, they are committed to helping others encounter God and receive His healing touch. Her prophetic heart brings a fresh connection to the Father's love.

She loves spending time with her husband and family. She plays on a competitive tennis league, enjoys running at the park and reading.

You can connect with Cindy, invite her for speaking engagements, or order her books and classes at:
 cindy@cindy-stewart.com

Her books are available on Amazon.com